FAITH
AN ADVENTURE TO BE EXPLORED

Alex and Lisa Snary

FAITH AN ADVENTURE TO BE EXPLORED
Copyright © 2021 by Alex and Lisa Snary

ISBN: 978-1-8384838-3-8

All rights reserved.
No part of this publication may be reproduced, stored in a retrieval system, or transmitted in any form or by any means, electronic, mechanical, photocopying or otherwise, without prior written consent of the publisher except as provided by under United Kingdom copyright law. Short extracts may be used for review purposes with credits given.

Main translation in use: Scripture quotations taken from The Holy Bible, New International Version® NIV® Copyright © 1973 1978 1984 2011 by Biblica, Inc. ™ Used by permission. All rights reserved worldwide.

Emphasis within Scripture quotations is the author's own.

Published by
Maurice Wylie Media
Your Inspirational Christian Publisher

Publishers' statement: Throughout this book the love for our God is such that whenever we refer to Him we honour with Capitals. On the other hand, when referring to the devil, we refuse to acknowledge him with any honour to the point of violating grammatical rule and withholding capitalisation.

For more information visit
www.MauriceWylieMedia.com

Contents

Introduction		**11**
Chapter 1	**Living life as a journey**	**15**
	Seeing life as a journey	
	Six days on a train	
	Trouble awaits us	
	Midnight on the docks in Tangier	
	Engaging in the moment	
Chapter 2	**Faith to Start**	**29**
	You must embrace the journey	
	Did someone mention a McDonalds?	
	Poker face pastor meets Alex	
	The test that we run from	
	Canvass wings and no seats	
	Eat or drink whatever your given	
Chapter 3	**Faith for God's Provision**	**54**
	Even God will look after the small things	
	Nothing prepares you for the real thing	
	Eating the dog's food	
	When there's no doctor nearby	
	Working amongst insurgencies	
	Finding courage in the midst of fear	
	South Sudan – Apocalypse now	
Chapter 4	**ATM Faith Machine**	**88**
	A Hebrew understanding of faith	
	Real Faith – An anchor in the storms of life	

| Chapter 5 | **Faith Lives Beyond Circumstances** | **95** |

Falling from the sky
Fake Faith versus Faith
Taken by Maoist Guerrillas
The key to focusing on God, not circumstances
An angel on each wing and two on the tail

| Chapter 6 | **Developing an Authentic Faith** | **109** |

Everest Base Camp
Stepping out in faith - A blind man healed
A picnic gone wrong
Smugglers for Jesus
Bloodshed and saving lives in a war zone
Letters with final goodbyes

| Chapter 7 | **Faith to trust God's decisions** | **133** |

Why God, why?

| Chapter 8 | **Faith and Suffering** | **146** |

The suffering of the innocent
Difficult questions
The cost of sin
Why does God not stop suffering?
With suffering there is hope
Riding with a message of hope
God in the midst of suffering
God's Love Abounds

Chapter 9 **God's Formula for Faith** **177**
Trust in the Lord with all of your heart
Lean not on your own understanding
In all of your ways submit to Him
And He will make your paths straight

Chapter 10 **A Supernatural Experience** **183**
Journey without end
Walking in faith
Available for adventure
Knowing who we journey with
Turn into God's voice

Contact details **197**

> *"There is meaning in every journey that is unknown to the traveller."*
> Dietrich Bonhoeffer

Dedication

There is always a cost to be paid when you make a journey, especially one that makes an impact along the way. While we have paid part of the cost ourselves, we are very aware that the cost has also been paid by key people in our lives. We dedicate this book to all those who have been so willing to contribute to this cost.

First, to our kids: who were so willing to go along with all the craziness. It's true the journey has made you who you are today, and we are so proud of you but there were also plenty of hardship and insecurity which have left scars.

To our wider family: for every birthday, Christmas and wedding we missed and for grandkids growing up apart from you. We couldn't have done it without your support and if you had not released us to follow where God was leading us.

To all those who over the years spiritually mentored us, supported us and upheld us in prayer: I know, without a doubt, we would not have survived as a family and would not be here to write this book, if you had not been faithfully covering us in prayer.

Finally, to all our dear friends and colleagues in the field: your hard work and dedication and willingness to sacrifice and even give your lives to make a difference in the lives of those who suffer, has been a constant inspiration to us. We know you will never receive the full acknowledgement you deserve in this lifetime, but be assured God sees all and it will not be forgotten.

Introduction

Life's a journey and this book comes out of the extraordinary journey the Lord has taken us on. Someone once described it as 'Indiana Jones meets Mother Teresa'. It's a journey that's lasted more than thirty years and covered more than sixty-five countries. It's a journey that's allowed us to see and experience the heights the human heart can rise to in expressing real *'rubber hits the road'* love, self-sacrifice and character; and the depths it can plunge into hatred, selfishness and depravity.

Every journey has its high and lows and our journey was no different. There were moments of extreme highs, when we were astounded at the extra ordinary things God was able to accomplish with our very ordinary talents and abilities, and moments of extreme lows when we felt lost and unsure. Those were the moments when we said "God, beam me up. I don't know what I'm doing here".

Throughout the highs and lows, the one constant has been faith: a faith which started out brash but fragile, and somehow through the journey has become perhaps more reflective and certainly more enduring.

What type of book is this? I have no idea how to fit it neatly into a box. I'm guessing you won't have read a book quite like this before, and may not again. It's wrapped around our unique journey away from the familiar into unexplored territory in our lives. It's about faith, because faith is developed as we step away from the familiar things in our lives and journey into new and unexplored territory.

For each person, what is 'unexplored territory' is different. It may be a new relationship, a new job or moving to a new city. For us it was literally moving around the world from one impoverished or disaster or conflict location to the next.

For many years people kept saying to us that we should write a book about our journey; but for a long time, we hesitated. We didn't want to write something that would just be entertaining, because that wouldn't respect the tremendous sacrifices made by our friends and colleagues who are part of our journey. We didn't want to write a book just about us, because the real story is not about us; it's about the One who saved us – Jesus Christ. So we decided to make faith the central theme, as it has been central throughout our journey.

We've used real stories from our journey to illustrate the lessons about faith that God has taught us along the way. All the stories are true. In some places some of the detail has been omitted in order to protect the privacy or reputation of individuals or organisations, or because years later our memory is not as clear as it once was; but it all happened.

The danger in using these often-extraordinary events is that the reader may be tempted to think these lessons about faith can only be learnt and applied if you go through extraordinary experiences. Of course, nothing could be further from the truth. We hope you realise that the real truth is, if God could develop our faith in such extreme circumstances, then He can certainly do the same for you in your situation.

Our hope and prayer is that, in reading this book, the part faith plays in your journey will be challenged. That you will dare to step out a bit more boldly, take a few more risks, and perhaps journey to a space you were fearing to tread and allow God to enlarge and grow your faith.

We've struggled together, triumphed together and discovered the lessons of faith together; and so we've tackled writing this book together.

So sit back, buckle up, and we pray that as you read this book, you will take a significant step forward in your own journey in faith.

Alex & Lisa Snary

CHAPTER 1

Living Life as a Journey

All journeys have a beginning and an end. As the Maoist Area Commander raged, his face inches from my own, screaming "why shouldn't I execute you right now", I realised, with a hollow sick feeling in my stomach, that my life's journey was rapidly coming to an end. I was 37 years old and Lisa was 35 years old.

My Nepali friend and colleague and I sat together on a log, armed guerrillas behind us with weapons trained on us, as the commander slammed a grenade down on the fragile card table in front of us. His angry tirade continued, and again and again he slammed his fist down on the card table, causing the grenade to leap and jump about like it had a life of its own. With a morbid fascination, my eyes locked on the grenade. I saw that instead of a split pin and safety bail, the only thing stopping it from popping was a rusty nail which was gradually working its way out every time it bounced on the table. Great, so now the only question was whether we were going to die by a bullet in the head or the grenade going off, splattering our bodies all over the place. Either way it looked like the end and I prayed "Jesus, here I come. I hope you're ready to catch me."

It was then my thoughts turned to my life's journey up until that point of time and all the places it had taken me to.

I was just like King Solomon when he was obsessed with figuring out what was the meaning of life.

Why was I born? Why at this time? What am I meant to do? Is there a divine plan for my life? If there is, then am I following it? Not only have these questions been asked for generations; they seem to be asked across all cultures and societies. I wonder: have you ever asked the same?

Life as a journey

As you move around the world, you discover that different cultures and different people groups have different worldviews. I've always found it interesting to see how different cultures deal with the questions around a person's life journey. Western culture is fixated on seeing life as a series of events and seeing a successful person as someone who is able to tick off the items on his bucket list. We are so preoccupied with worrying about how to manage future events that we never have time to fully experience the here and now.

In contrast, I have found that other cultures such as the Middle East see life as a journey, as something to be enjoyed, to be savoured. The journey, the here and now is what's important, not some future destination.

In a similar way, I've found in the Middle East that spirituality is not defined in terms of a series of destinations to be reached, but rather as an ongoing daily journey that takes you deeper within yourself and deeper in relationship with God.

At one stage of our journey... I was working in the West Bank and went to the village of one of my Christian Palestinian co-workers to celebrate a local wedding. Palestinian weddings are huge affairs with lots of people, lots of food and compulsory dancing until dawn, whether you consider yourself a dancer or not!

Carried on and on by the wild tempo of the music, the laughter and cheers, I tromped across the room, arms in the air, showing more enthusiasm than skill. As true exhaustion began to set in and my arms and legs cried "enough!", I collapsed into a chair at a table with some of the older men from the village. From the broken bits of Arabic I could follow, I gathered they were laughing and joking about some of the life lessons the young couple would have to learn; starting with the wedding night, and the issue of whether the groom had drunk too much to do his duty!

I began to reflect on how, despite more than sixty years of military occupation and oppression, the Palestinian people really know how to celebrate. They have a zest for life that's infectious. They are passionately connected to each other, their past and their land. They have a sense of who they are and where they belong. They understand how each person's individual journey connects to the journey of those who have gone before and how their children will carry it on.

As the music lost its frantic pace and a haunting melody began, the topic of conversation among the older men turned to things more spiritual, as it so often does there. Talking with one of the men who had been educated in the United States and who spoke great English, I foolishly asked him when he had accepted Jesus Christ as his Lord and Saviour, thinking it may have been when he was studying. He told me...

"Well, it began when Jesus was travelling from Galilee to Jerusalem and stayed the night with his disciples in our village. Our forefathers believed his message and became followers of Jesus and that's when our journey as believers began."

With my western mind-set I was looking for an event, when what was important was a journey which began 2000 years ago and was continuing on in the present day in the lives of these villagers.

The best journeys are not ones in which we see the journey as a series of events or tasks to be completed but rather as an adventure to be explored, where we stay in the moment as the journey unfolds before us, not quite sure what's around the next corner; and one which perhaps connects our past with who we will be in the future.

In 1996 we were living and working in the Mongolian countryside, implementing aid and development projects and leading a small church. After two years living in difficult conditions with -30°C winters, we were both quite exhausted and our leader told us we needed to take a break.

We hadn't planned on taking a break then and didn't have any plans in place; so we decided to just set out on a journey. We would just go until either our leave period or money ran out.

We decided to jump on a train and head west. We weren't sure exactly where we were going, what we would find along the way or where we would end up. We would explore and just be in the moment. For six days we travelled over 7,600km from Ulaanbaatar to Moscow in what turned out to be THE train experience of a lifetime: we wondered at the vast frozen emptiness of the Siberian landscape with its endless snowy forests, and the unforgettable crazy cook who would suddenly burst out of his kitchen yelling and frantically waving a meat cleaver; the regular punch-ups in the dining car when everyone became sufficiently tanked on cheap vodka. Gradually with the click clack click clack of the train and the endless forest passing the window, we began to relax, and to stop asking how much longer to Moscow and just enjoy the moment.

Six days on a train...

Lisa... *That train ride was something else. The thought of six days on a train in a small, tiny room was daunting: how would we cope? It turns out the train ride had its own unique entertainment. Mongolian people are some of the most innovative people I know. The journey was fascinating. We shared a room with one other person who spoke little English but I'll never forget as he started unpacking his bag and pulling the panels off the walls to hide items like jeans, sports shoes, cutlery etc. and then cover it up with the panel. He had us stand so he could put jeans under our mattress and he even motioned for us to put stuff in our bags, but we refused.*

We only realised when we got to the border that this stuff was being hidden from the Russia customs officials to smuggle it across the border to sell. Once across the border, when we made stops along the way, he would bring out all the stuff from behind the panels and out of his bags and hang out of the window doing a roaring trade. As we looked out our window, all the way up and down the train you could see Mongols doing the same thing, calling out the items they had for sale. You name it, they pretty much had everything and anything any Russian buyer wanted.

Those six days on the train were amazing. We experienced the most incredible scenery. If you've ever seen the movie Dr Zhivago, where they take the train through the Russian countryside, that was the scene we got to take in; and all this punctuated by the regular 'window' marketplace and the occasional restaurant car brawl! As Alex said, it was an unforgettable experience.

From Moscow, we decided to continue through Poland and Germany to the United Kingdom, then France and Spain, and finally ended up in Morocco before our time and money ran out and we had to return home.

The journey was full of unexpected delights. After surviving for two years in Mongolia on meat and a bit of rice and flour, the mouth-watering food in the French markets was heaven on earth. It was full of tasty cheeses and fine wine, everything our stomachs could imagine. Each meal was an exploration of new gastronomic delights.

In Spain we discovered paella and the beautiful beaches of the southern Spanish coast. Warm sun and lazy swims with afternoon siestas and evening tapas were exactly what we needed.

We managed to get ourselves into a bit of trouble when we decided to go to a flamenco night at one of the villages nearby. Being fairly ignorant of Spanish culture, we thought flamenco was only about guitars and dancing. So sitting waiting expectantly for the dancers to appear, we were totally surprised when a very old unshaven gent made his way unsteadily to the front, grabbed the microphone and launched into song.

If you've ever heard flamenco singing, it's very distinctive. We mistakenly thought the village drunk guy had hijacked the concert. For some reason, which I cannot for the life of me remember, we found this totally hilarious and began to collapse in hysterical peals of laughter. Gradually through the tears of laughter, we saw the entire square of people was now looking at us in shock, horror and most of all, anger. As an angry local demanded "what makes you think you can come as a foreigner to our village and disrespect a national treasure of Spain? " we suddenly realised our foolish mistake. Oh no! We had suddenly become one of those loud insensitive tourists we hated so much. With much apologising, we beat a hasty retreat, before the thoughts of the villagers could turn to lynching or stoning or whatever they do to ignorant foreigners who are totally disrespectful to one of the greatest flamenco singers of all time: a living national treasure of Spain. Not our finest hour!

Deciding it was time to move on, we crossed the Mediterranean to Morocco and were totally captivated by the wonder of the Medina in the ancient city of Marrakech. By day it looks similar to other North African cities, but at night, the Medina transforms to an Ali Baba wonderland, with snake charmers, ancient water sellers, and wise men reading the stars. Local street hawkers and merchants try to sell you everything from chameleons to copper oil lamps (yes, with a genie included for no extra price!) and jokingly asking how many camels for your pretty wife (actually, years later, I learned a difficult lesson about how serious the trafficking of women is in this region, when I accidentally almost sold the beautiful Marketing Director of the organisation I worked for to an old Bedouin and his sons. We were travelling together, and I thought we were all joking when he started to enquire what the price would be for her; but it turned out he was deadly serious and very insistent that I honour the deal. Guys: never, never, never joke about selling a woman).

Trouble awaits us…

There were other unexpected challenges as well. On the train travelling from Russia to Germany through Poland, we managed to get into trouble at the Polish border. We had met a guy from Canada who was sharing our cabin. As we were talking, the conversation turned to the high cost of visas. Apparently, in Moscow he had been charged $300 for a Polish visa and was not even planning to stop over in Poland. We were confused: why get a visa at all? Then it hit us: this was a train, not a plane. We were so used to travelling by plane and being in transit in the countries we passed through, that we hadn't realised on a train there is no such thing as transit.

Wow! The Canadian guy was saying "I can't imagine how much this will cost you in fines and visa costs to get this cleared up at the border".

Given our very limited travel budget, we began to alternate between panic and prayer.

Sure enough, when we reached the Polish border, the Polish officials boarded the train and demanded to see our passports and visas. When I tried to explain, I was immediately marched off the train by unimpressed, jackbooted border guards. What was going to happen? Where was I being taken? The guards spoke no English. As I was marched away, I told Lisa to stay on the train and contact the embassy in Germany. My escort and I eventually arrived in a small grimy, smoke-stained brick office, and I was told to sit by an old Soviet-style metal desk. The official drew another long pull on his cigarette and slowly reached into the desk drawer. With a flood of relief, I saw him pull out visa stamps and begin to flick through the pages of my passport. Slowly he began to issue visas for the three of us. As he finished, he began to question his colleagues and then pointed to our Mongolian visa and the $20 written in the corner of the visa. He asked was this USD? I realised he'd probably never seen a New Zealand passport and wasn't sure how much to charge. Finally, he said "twenty dollars". With a great amount of cheek given the circumstances I replied "twenty dollars for three?" and with that, the deal was done. Twenty dollars for three visas!

I rushed back to the train, thanking Jesus all the way. In the end the officials were happy we had the necessary visas, we were happy it was at a cost we could afford, and everyone was happy. Oh - except for the Canadian guy, who almost cried when he learnt we'd managed to get THREE visas for only twenty dollars.

London was suffering a full-on heat wave and it wasn't even summer. It was hot and sticky in a country not used to heat and not set up for it. We had come out of frozen Mongolia and we also were not prepared for it. We tramped around London sweating looking for somewhere to hang out in the cool.

Now in Mongolia there was no such thing as travellers' cheques; and Visa cards were unheard of. We had become used to dealing in cash: the USA dollar is a kind of international currency in Central Asia. I was carrying about $2,000 dollars on me, which was most of our total holiday money. With all of the talk of travellers being robbed on trains, I had worked out that I could remove the inner soles of my hiking boots and stash the cash secretly there. Which was all good; until we walked around London sweating in the heat. After a week I thought I should just check the cash in my boots. To my horror, I discovered the cash was destroyed! It had gotten damp and in addition, there were perforated holes all through it from the pattern on the sole of the boots. It was a disaster! What were we going to do? How are we going to get home?

There we were with no place to stay and our money trashed. We sat down outside the train station not knowing what to do, praying "God, what now?" Just then an elderly, scruffy-looking woman in a dirty trench coat came up to me and pressed a crumpled-up card into my hand. I was just about to chuck it away when I caught the word 'accommodation' written on it.

"Great! What use is accommodation with no money to pay for it, God? And anyway, who would take the recommendation of a homeless woman on where to spend the night, unless we were planning to sleep on the street?" I said to myself, muttering.

Then, breaking through our whining and complaining, Lisa and I felt a prompting in our spirits to go to the address on the card and check it out. Maybe God could use a homeless woman and a crumpled card to answer our prayers. Using some of our small pile of remaining cash, we took a bus to the address on the card, expecting the worst but hoping for a miracle.

We arrived at a three-storied terraced house in a poor neighbourhood. The door banged open and we were almost bowled over by a shrieking group of punk rockers complete with safety pins in their ears, noses and lips and swastikas tattooed on their faces.

As they jumped and shouted their way past us and down the street, we were more convinced than ever this was a mistake; then we saw a small cross in the window. It somehow seemed to be beckoning us to come in.

Inside, there was the beautiful smell of home cooking and we were greeted by a lovely older couple who greeted us as if we were long lost family with hugs all around.

It turned out that they were believers who opened their home for people to stay. We explained our situation and we were assured there was no need to worry about the money: we could sort that out later. The house was packed with people, but they found space for us squeezed up in the attic.

The next day the miracles continued. We received a message from friends who were living in China. They had heard we were in London and wanted us to know they had family just outside London who would love to have us to stay for a few days, if we could manage it.

Manage it …. too right we could manage it!

We met with the older couple to work out a way to settle our bill for the night, but they refused to charge us anything. Instead, they gave us scripture cards to hand out along the way. Such beautiful generous people. Angels in disguise? Who knows?

With the last of our cash, we managed to buy train tickets to the suburb where the family of our friends in China lived. Not only did this family insist we stayed with them, but it turned out that the wife worked in a bank and she was able to take our smudged, tattered notes with the tears and holes all through them and replace them with brand new crisp notes.

We were good to go once more. Thank you, God!

Midnight on the docks in Tangier…

As delightful as our experience of Marrakech in Morocco was, the same cannot be said for the Moroccan trains or our experience of the docks in Tangier. Mindful of our budget, we had travelled to Marrakech in a third-class carriage. The experience had been a bit like being boiled in a sardine can: hot, sweaty, sticky bodies packed in together. Our body odour mixed with everyone else's body odour to transform the atmosphere from life giving oxygen to something acridly pungent which left you gasping for breath.

It was a full day journey, and we weren't excited about returning to Tangier in the same hot overcrowded carriage. So, we decided to treat ourselves to an upgrade and bought second-class tickets, where we were assured the carriages had full air conditioning and only one person to a seat. Wow, such luxury! We couldn't wait, and hurried to the platform.

There we found a sea of humanity surrounding our train. People, baggage, more people, carts, still more people. People were crammed around each carriage entrance. People were shouting everywhere; people were being passed over the crowd. It was total chaos. There was nothing for it but to dive into the press and make our way to the train. With some determined pushing and shoving, we managed to force our way to the nearest carriage entrance. Over the din of hundreds of people shouting, I tried to ask the harried conductor where the second-class AC carriage was. "AC? Okay, follow me" he said, took us and sat us between the carriages. "Train start, AC come" he said with a grin as he disappeared back inside. With a laugh, we propped our backpacks against the rail and made ourselves comfortable, deciding to go with it. Actually, sitting with our legs dangling over the edge and the warm Moroccan breeze in our faces, it wasn't a bad ride.

The trip took a lot longer than scheduled, though, and that's where our real challenge started. We were due to arrive in Tangier mid-afternoon, which would give us time to find a place to stay before dark. We'd been warned not to hang around the port after dark, as local gangs who preyed on tourists were common. Violent muggings, extortion, kidnapping and trafficking apparently were all part of the scene at the docks.

By the time the train pulled into the port where we needed to get off, it was almost midnight. Midnight on the docks in Tangier… not good. Sure enough, it wasn't long before we attracted the wrong kind of attention. A gang of four or five young toughs began to follow us. We hurried around a corner and positioned ourselves with our backs to a building entrance. We unpacked our arsenal ready to do battle. Out came my six-inch switchblade, and Lisa's taser and can of mace.

Probably some kind of explanation is needed at this point. Why were we travelling armed to the teeth? At this time Russia was still going through some major transitions, and it could be dangerous travelling through some parts of Russia. We had been advised to make sure that we were able to take care of ourselves, should we run into trouble. When we got to Morocco, we were still carrying an assortment of weaponry: which, of course, these days since 911, you could never get away with; but back then when traveling by train, it was possible.

The gang came running around the corner and came to an abrupt halt finding their victims ready for them and at least as well armed as they were. There were some hasty, urgent whispers back and forth and then they walked nonchalantly past us, pretending they were never even slightly interested in us. I guess they'd decided to look for easier pickings. Thank you, Lord, for stepping in once again and delivering us from what could have been a very nasty situation, had they decided to make a fight of it or been better armed.

One thing about our journey together is it has always had its crazy but scary moments; and this was definitely one of them. When Alex told me we needed to carry weapons on this trip, and then we had to be prepared for a possible clash in Tangier with gangs of drug addicts, I felt nervous and afraid, especially as we had spoken with a couple on the way who had had a bad run in with a group of men on the docks in Tangier. We knew our God was faithful and should we have any trouble, He would be with us; we also went prepared. Hiding in the alleyway had my heart pounding as that group of guys came around the corner. I was praying that nothing would come of that incident. I thank the Lord that he gave me Alex as my husband; he always just seemed to know how to handle such situations.

Engaging in the Moment

All of this, both the good and the bad, made for a memorable journey; but what made this trip so special was that we were fully engaged in the moment. We didn't know where we were going or what was coming next; we just lived life day to day, fully absorbing each day's delights and challenges.

Our spiritual journey should be the same. We should be fully engaged each day with where God has led us TODAY. What is God wanting to teach me TODAY? What area is God wanting me to grow in TODAY? What am I struggling with that I need to take to God TODAY? What is God wanting to bless me with TODAY?

By remaining in the here-and-now, we squeeze everything there is to be had from our relationship with God.

This is particularly important as we go on to discuss our journey in faith. Our faith grows in steps: sometimes baby steps and sometimes giant leaps; but always in steps. There is no short cut, and each step is important. If we miss a step, it usually means that God has to bring us back to the same place once again, because each step leads to the next. It's all about the process, all about the journey and there are no shortcuts in the faith journey.

CHAPTER 2
Faith to Start

Finding the courage to start a journey can be a real challenge. We are creatures of habit. We like our comfort zone where everything is familiar, and we think we have everything under control. Thirty years into our ministry journey, we have friends who had the same passion and felt the same pull of God to set their feet on the path of ministry that we felt. But they never made a start. They could never bring themselves to take the first stumbling steps. They've found one reason after another to hesitate. "We want to get ourselves financially stable first. Then we have a mortgage and are starting a new business." Then later "there are a few health issues now which we need to work through."

I'm not saying buying a house, starting a business or dealing with health issues are wrong. They are normal things couples do. It's only an issue if it becomes a barrier to your fulfilling the purpose God has for your life; if it's the thing you hide behind because it's too scary to start a journey into the unknown. If all we had to rely on was our personal courage, most of us would never start journeys that could take us well outside our comfort zones.

This is where faith comes in. Faith is different from courage. When we're struggling to screw up the courage to do something, our thoughts are all about whether we can do this; whether we have what it takes, whether we can we push forward, and wondering if we will be successful and complete the journey.

When we step out in faith, all of these dynamics shift. It's no longer about me, it's all about Him. We no longer wrestle with fears and doubts on the shifting sand of our own strengths and abilities. We take comfort in the solid rock of our all-powerful, almighty God, knowing that if He's called us, then He's got this in hand.

This reminds me of a journey I once made by jeep from Ulaanbaatar, the capital of Mongolia, to Onderkhan, the Regional capital of the Khentee province. It was a 400km cross-country trip and I was determined to drive it rather than hire a vehicle or go by post truck. Driving cross-country in Mongolia is a unique experience. In the 1990's, the only roads were close to the capital; everywhere else you made your own road. Local drivers navigated their way by landmarks such as mountains and rivers (which on the steppe are few and far between). My Mongolian co-worker wasn't a driver and neither of us knew the landmarks to get there safely. My plan was to use an old map I'd found, and my trusty compass.

Looking back, it was kind of crazy I admit; but I was confident because of the navigation skills that had been drilled into me in my five years as an officer in the New Zealand Army. My time in the military would be up to the task. Even more than this, I had a sense God was in this trip and would really use us, if we would trust Him. My co-worker was not so confident, however, and his wife was in a panic. She was sure we would disappear into the Mongolian steppe, never to return. She called me the night before we were due to leave. She was in tears, sobbing and begging me not to take her husband on such a journey.

Looking back now I know it was kind of crazy, and it would have been easy to cancel the trip and stay in the relative warmth and safety of the capital, but if we had done this, we would have missed so much.

The trip was one of the richest experiences in my twelve years in Mongolia. It wasn't without its challenges. The first was when, only a couple of hours into the journey, the Mongolian guy we had brought with us to help with breakdowns and navigation, admitted he hadn't actually ever been to Onderkhan. At one stage, while trying to cross a flooded river, we fell into a sinkhole and water came flooding into the vehicle. We were sitting in the vehicle with water up to our waists and could hear the fan chopping the water like a propeller. We were half out of the water with bubbles coming out of the exhaust. Then the engine died. One thing about Russian jeeps is that while they need constant maintenance, they are really hard to kill and easy to resurrect. Fortunately, the water level was just below the tube for the dipstick and it hadn't completely flooded into the engine. By putting it into first gear and using the starter motor, we managed to bunny-hop the jeep into shallower water. The engine started once again, much to our surprise. We drove up onto the bank and opened the doors, letting the water pour out and set off again.

The Mongolian steppe is hard to describe because it's difficult to find words that adequately capture its vastness. Unless you've experienced it, whatever words I use will cause you to visualise something too small and too confined.

Except for the millions of stars, the huge blue, blue sky turns to complete blackness at night. It is almost as if there are more stars than empty space. The rolling grasslands have absolutely no landmarks. It's a vast untouched land without fences. There is nothing to close you in. No signs of human habitation can be seen, except for the very occasional line of telephone poles or tyre tracks. Raw nature is all around: a hawk feeding on a carcass; a marmot poking his head out of his hole to watch you go by. All around is a vastness that by its very nature resists the encroachment of humanity. The few herdsmen that live there, do so in the only way that works. They live in their gers (felt tents) much the same way their ancestors did in the days of Chinggis Khaan. They live there on the land's terms, not their own: a nomadic lifestyle, dictated by land and climate.

You must embrace the journey

That trip was special in so many ways. Up until then I had resisted Mongolia. I'd felt out of place. I was a stranger in a strange land. On that trip, I embraced Mongolia, and she embraced me. Something touched my soul which has never left me. Even now, when I open my old Bible and smell the sheep fat on the pages, or I hear something on the television about Mongolia, my heart starts to beat a bit faster and I feel again, her vast presence.

All this happened as I engaged with the land, the people and the culture. It happened through the bonds of friendship and brotherhood with the Mongolian guys as we laughed, wrestled and rode horses together. The physical demands of the lifestyle bonds you to the land and to each other. At one stage we rode for more than 15km at the canter, while herding horses.

Even though my thighs and backside had been rubbed raw (literally bleeding raw) by the hard-wooden Mongolian saddle, I was elated that I'd been able to keep up with the others. As we rode back to camp, they slapped me on the back laughing and joking … not bad for a foreigner. Of course, this turned to absolute hysterics for them when, on reaching the camp I tried to dismount, only to find my numb legs wouldn't support me and I collapsed in the mud like a turtle on its back and couldn't move.

It was a pivotal time. After this experience, my relationship with Mongolia and its people was never the same. Something had shifted in my spirit. I moved from being in Mongolia as an act of obedience because God had called me there, to being in Mongolia because I loved Mongolia. This change became a transition in the spirit realm; the difference between going and being sent. I loved the Mongolian people, and God had called me there.

All of this happened as a result of taking the step to move beyond the fear of starting a journey; and trusting God, that He would be with us as we journeyed.

The origins of my own spiritual journey to faith are clouded in the haze of pain that comes from growing up in a home with an angry, abusive father, in a family which finally split apart when I was 14 years old. My father had grown up with an abusive father and history repeated itself. He would sit me down and seriously lecture me, telling me "When you're married don't be too weak to give your wife a good beating now and then. They all need it." It was something he also applied to my brother and me, seemingly at random.

Finally, my mother had enough and filed for divorce. My father left and took my younger brother with him. I stayed to look after Mum. Life was difficult and money was tight, but at least there was peace at home. It was a peace we had never known. I watched other kids play sports and go on family holidays, while I worked at the small shop Mum ran. I became angry at my world and had a huge chip on my shoulder. I was always in scraps at school, happy to take a swing at anyone who looked at me sideways. Whether in school or out of school, trouble always seems to be there. The constant fighting that had been happening in my home when my Father was there, had now manifested in my life.

I tried to numb the pain with drink and partying. I tried filling the hole in my heart with a series of disastrous relationships and one-night stands; but each one just left me more emotionally cut up and bleeding. I didn't know what I needed; but I knew I was searching. Was this it?

Was this all there was to life? What was the point? Who was I and did my life have any meaning?

I had started learning martial arts at the suggestion of one of my teachers, after I half killed a kid at school. The only reason I wasn't expelled was that the kid was a major bully and had trained as a boxer; and so I think the teachers thought it was fair enough. My teacher warned me that I couldn't keep losing it; and if I did, I would end up in serious trouble. So I took up martial arts to learn to channel my anger and aggression in more positive and controlled ways.

Martial arts helped me get some control, but it didn't deal with the pain inside. I tried Buddhism and got into Zen, looking for peace in emptiness but all I found was …… emptiness. I didn't want emptiness, I wanted healing, I wanted wholeness, I wanted to believe in something real, I wanted to have faith in someone or something that wouldn't abandon me, wouldn't let me down, wouldn't use and abuse me. Then I was hit by two life-changing events that came one after another.

For anyone who has ever played air hockey… the disc floats on a table of air jets and you whack it back and forth trying to score. The disc careens off the handle and the sides of the table and when it connects, it radically changes direction and shoots off at speed. That's what happened to me. I got hit with a double whammy that radically changed the direction of my life when I met Lisa and I met God.

God had to work very hard to get us together. Without God, it would never have been possible.

Did someone mention a McDonalds?

It's embarrassing, but yes, we met at McDonalds. When we started going out together, our friends couldn't believe it. I was so unstable that at our wedding our friends had a bet going about how many months our marriage might last. We were so different. Lisa was a born-again believer. She had morals and ethics. She came from a real family, a family that despite its challenges, actually functioned as family. At that time, I knew nothing about how a family should function

In the beginning, I thought it wasn't Lisa and me that were supposed to get together. A friend of mine was totally smitten with Lisa. He was desperate to go out with her and had tried everything he could think of to get her to notice him. One night over a few drinks, actually quite a few drinks, he told me of his dilemma; and in a rush of alcohol-induced misguided brilliance, we came up with what we considered to be the perfect scheme, worthy of Cupid himself. He would try the old-fashioned romantic approach. To our beer-befuddled brains it was a sure thing. Flowers, chocolates and poetry, lots of poetry. Everyone knows the poet always gets the girl (something he should have taken more note of, as it turned out).

Anyway, it looked like a winner. Except for one thing… my friend couldn't write a decent poem to save himself or the love of his life. Like a drowning man reaching for a soggy biscuit to keep himself afloat, he assured me that I was a natural poet and would do a brilliant job. I've no idea how he figured I could do this, when the closest I had come to writing anything was penning a few soppy lyrics to a couple of songs to sing in pubs on Saturday nights, to make a few bucks. So it was settled. He would get the flowers and chocolates each week and each week I would produce a poem guaranteed to melt the heart of fair Lisa. There are a lot of very good reasons not to drink to excess, and crazy schemes like this are just one of them.

We set the scheme in motion. Chocolates, poems, flowers, poems; at first it was all good: he seemed to be getting her attention. Unfortunately, in the end the kind of attention he got was not what he was looking for.

I headed back home for the summer and he was forced to improvise his own poetry. He was right about one thing: he could NOT write romantic poetry. Not only was his poetry not romantic, his poor range of romantic vocabulary meant that it was kind of, well… xxx rated. It was the kind of thing that makes a girl think she's being chased by a crazed stalker, the kind of thing that brings her six-foot, hundred kg, and over-protective father coming, looking to break something over someone's head. It was over. The truth came out; and we were busted. So, while my friend decided that a broken heart was much preferable to having other body parts broken and gave up his pursuit of fair Lisa, it didn't end all that badly because, as in all good tales, once again, the poet got the girl.

Lisa and I started going out together and after only a few months, we got engaged. It was romantic bliss but, just like having a pebble in your new pair of Reeboks, Lisa's Mum and I kept fighting about God. We would go at it hammer and tongs. I kept telling her God was a figment of her imagination or a crutch for the emotionally weak or an opiate for the masses, but she kept on staunchly testifying to the reality of what God had done in her life.

Poker face pastor meets Alex

We would be at it for hours. There were times when Lisa, in total frustration, would go out and come back a couple of hours later; and we hadn't even noticed she had left. Finally, she had enough and declared that a truce must be put in place. Like all truces, there was a list of conditions for each party to abide by. Lisa's Mum would cease and desist all further conversations about God; and I would agree to go and talk out my issues about God with a pastor. The future of our relationship would hang on the success of the cease-fire.

With so much at stake, I dutifully went to talk with the pastor BUT I was determined it wasn't going to be an easy conversation for him. I went locked and loaded with all of my arguments and complaints against religion and the idea of God fully rehearsed.

As soon as I was seated in his office, and with all the arrogance of my 20 years, I went on the attack. Smoothly rolling from one argument to the next, I hammered him with one set of reasoning after another, like guided missiles, passionately explaining, beyond a shadow of a doubt, why God couldn't be real.

The intensity of my verbal assault was such that he hadn't been able to respond or refute anything so far (in fact he hadn't been able to get a word in to say anything). I paused to draw breath and congratulate myself on how well this was going.

That's when it came: the verbal ankle tap that completely threw me. I had experienced the same feeling in my youth: running flat out for the try-line with the rugby ball tucked tightly under my arm, thinking I was home free; when you feel the tap that connects with your ankle, causing you to lose all coordination and bringing you crashing to the ground. Same feeling...... same result.

All he said was "Do you want to meet God? Can I pray for you now?"

It wasn't so much what he said, as the way he said it. With such a quiet confidence. The reality crashed in on me, with the realisation that not only had nothing I had said made a dent in this man's faith, but he was willing to put his faith totally on the line. He was all in. Like a gambler pushing all his chips forward, he raised the stakes and was ready to lay his cards on the table; challenging me to do the same. He quietly but firmly explained that arguing about God was pointless... much better for me to meet him for myself.

This was crazy. Hadn't he heard me explain in great detail there was no God that I didn't believe in God? He's bluffing with a poker-face, I thought. He has to be. Alright then; I would call his bluff. He could pray for me and when no one responded to his prayers, it would be clear there was no one out there to respond. It would be clear his faith was a sham.

With a confident smirk on my face, I stood and let him gently place his hand on my shoulder.

I'm still to this day a bit fuzzy about what happened next. What I do know is that I woke up on the floor sometime later, knowing beyond any possible doubt that I had met the living God. There was no question in my mind that God was real, and He was the one I had been searching for. To make sure I got the message, I also somehow forgot how to speak English. I would open my mouth and these strange words would come pouring out like a flooding torrent. Rather than feel panic-stricken that I was totally losing it… it somehow felt right. I felt more whole inside.

The pastor kindly explained this was the work and gifting of the Holy Spirit. I thanked him and jumped on my motorbike to race to tell Lisa what had happened. As I regained the power of normal speech, I kept checking to see if this new heavenly language was still there. Each time my helmet would fill with the sound of wondrous new words and phrases, and my spirit would lift: something that continues to this day.

Each one of us has the choice to live life in the natural, pursuing our own short-lived agendas and blown by every wind of circumstance; or to encounter and embrace God, placing our feet on the path to a supernatural journey, carefully scripted by our loving Creator.

Like the explorers and adventurers of old, we can sit passively clinging to what we think we know, or we can screw up our courage and set sail on a journey of spiritual discovery that will transform how we understand the world around us and, in the process, transform us.

Just because it's a spiritual journey, doesn't mean it's for the faint-hearted. It can take every bit as much faith mixed with courage and commitment as those journeys of the early explorers.

I remember when our journey took us to the point of knowing that God was calling us to follow Him to serve internationally; and that our spiritual journey would continue away from the comfortable shores of our home in Aotearoa, New Zealand.

I had first felt a calling in this direction eight years previously while on our honeymoon in Fiji. We had arranged to stay in a tourist resort on Plantation Island. It was beautiful. The sea was beautiful, the beach was beautiful, the food was beautiful, and the staff were beautiful. Unfortunately, like a twisted version of 'Paradise Lost', the boatloads of loud, obnoxious tourists spoiled this paradise.

After a couple of days listening to constant complaints about how everything wasn't like home, I'd had enough. I mean really… wasn't the point to be somewhere not like home? Hadn't they paid thousands of dollars to get away from their miserable lives at home and now they were determined to bring that misery to paradise? After failing to come up with a cunning plan to get them away from the island, I decided the next best thing was for me to get away. So I did. I apologised to Lisa and went bush-heading into the jungle interior of the island.

I had no idea where I was going, I just needed to find some peace. I travelled most of the day deep into the jungle. Without a map or compass, I didn't know exactly where I was, but I felt confident that I could find my way by heading downhill and following the shoreline, so I wasn't worried. The peace of the jungle had begun to seep into my spirit, and I had begun to feel I could breathe again, when I heard what sounded faintly like singing. I climbed further and came upon a small foot-trail. As I followed it, I could hear the singing more clearly. It was absolutely beautiful. I rushed along the path and came upon a hut with a cross on top. The roof was thatched, the walls made of mud, and there was no door; but it was packed with local villagers. I quietly squeezed into the back, not wanting to disturb the service.

The singing and talking was all in Fijian. I couldn't understand anything that was being said; but as I took it all in, I felt God began to speak to me. For the first time, I felt the gentle tug on my spirit pulling me towards new spiritual shores. I began to understand that the course He had plotted for us would take us away from our life and careers in New Zealand, to minister internationally to the poorest and most vulnerable.

We returned home, and I couldn't wait to tell our pastor what God had spoken to me. I had checked and there was a short Missions course we could do, and in six months we could be out there making a difference. Fortunately for us, our pastor was an old-school, experienced missionary with years of experience of dealing with keen young couples. He had a deep understanding of the calling of God and what it takes to see it through.

He understood a great truth. From the time we hear the calling of God to when it becomes a reality in our lives, there is a journey to travel. It seems God will often require us to release the calling back to him and allow him to resurrect it in his perfect time. This journey, between hearing the call and it becoming a reality, takes faith. Faith to hold on to what God has spoken. Faith to keep it alive in our hearts.

The test we run from

Faith (or lack of faith) and calling seem to go hand in hand. In the Bible we see this starkly contrasted in the difference between the way Mary and Zechariah respond to the promise of God.

When Mary hears she's going to give birth to a son, her response in Luke 1:38 is **"I am the Lord's servant… may it be to me as you have said"** but when Zechariah hears his wife is to have a son, he doubts the Word of the Lord in Luke 1:18 **"How can I be sure of this? I am an old man, and my wife is well along in years"**. His lack of faith results in him being struck dumb until the coming of his son.

This delay is a time of testing. God tests whether our desire for the promise of His calling is greater than our trust and desire for Him. If our desire for God, our desire for relationship with Him, is not greater than our desire for the things He has promised to give us, then we have a problem; because it means we don't have a real relationship with Him, and we are only in it for what we can get out of it. Ever have a friend who only wanted to know you because of what they could get from you?

The journey is also a time of preparation to ensure we are prepared and ready to step into our calling. When God was ready to rescue the Israelites out of slavery in Egypt, He called them to enter into a promised land, a land flowing with milk and honey.

'And I have promised to bring you up out of your misery in Egypt into the land of the Canaanites, Hittites, Amorites, Perizzites, Hivites and Jebusites--a land flowing with milk and honey.' Exodus 3:17

But when they arrived at the river Jordan, where they were to enter into the land, they doubted God; they were fearful of entering the land. Their eyes were on how large and powerful the people of the land were, not on how powerful their God was. They rebelled against Moses and wanted to return to Egypt. They were not ready to enter into the calling of God.

WORKING WITH SYRIAN REFUGUEES IN JORDAN 2016

So God told Moses to take them back into the wilderness for 40 years. It took another 40 years for them to be prepared to fulfil the purposes God had for them.

For us to be able to enter into the call of God, we need to be ready. Our hearts need to be ready. We need to be trained, skilled and prepared for the tasks ahead, to go forward with the right attitude. Otherwise, we carry fatal flaws like hidden fault lines, which, under the pressure of the journey, crack open and cause us to fall.

It was eight years from the time we sensed the call of God on our lives, until we began our international ministry. While it was often a frustrating journey and we weren't clear where we would end up, we are so grateful for that time of preparation. If we had not been prepared to journey through these eight years, it would have been a disaster. During that time, God strengthened our faith: he trained us, and we worked out issues in our lives and in our marriage.

We saw what happened in the lives of those who were not adequately prepared.

When we were in Mongolia, we worked with a European colleague, who felt God calling her to move to the far north to work with the Tsaatan people, or the reindeer people, as they're known. The Tsaatan are reindeer herders who live up high in the mountainous northern part of Mongolia. They live in skin tents similar to the traditional teepees of Native American people in temperatures as low as -50°C and are very isolated. All people living in the countryside in Mongolia are somewhat isolated, but these people are extremely isolated. For part of each winter, it's not possible to travel to them.

Although our colleague planned to set up in a small hut in a small community down the mountain by a lake called Tsagaan Nuur (white lake) and work with another American woman, she was still going to be very isolated. Our leader, a very experienced Chinese missionary, was concerned that she was not yet ready for the extreme challenge of living and working in such conditions.

However, our colleague was insistent. She went back to her home country, raised the financial support she needed, bought a container load of gear and shipped it to Mongolia; all despite the misgivings of our leader.

When she was ready to depart, our leader asked us if we would go with her and help her get set up and make sure at least she had a safe, secure base to work from.

Canvas wings and no seats...

So we found ourselves loading up her gear into the back of a 1947 canvas biplane in one of our most bizarre Mongolian countryside adventures. Because this area was so isolated, we needed to take everything she was going to need. There were no local shops to buy goods. Everything had to be brought in with us. This included wood sheets and building materials and tools to fix up her hut, furnishings, food and medical supplies: everything she would need to get through the winter until she could make it down for a spring resupply. To fit all the gear into the old biplane, the pilot had taken out all of the seats. We loaded the gear in, and lay down on top of it, with our noses inches from the roof.

One of the things you quickly learn about canvas biplanes, is that they fly the same way a cork floats, bouncing and bobbing their way through the sky. With our visibility limited to the roof above our faces and the plane jumping at every thermal, it was hard to know what was going on. The only reference I had was the time since take off. So it came as a total shock when only half way into the trip and after one particularly large bounce, the cockpit door was forced open and the two pilots crawled quickly over the gear, opened the door and jumped out.

What was happening? Were we going down? Who was flying the plane? Making our way to the door, we were shocked to see grass. We were on the ground. We must have crash-landed. Imagining the effects of exploding engines in a canvas biplane, I yelled for everyone to get out and run for it. We ran from the plane expecting the plane to go up at any minute. But that was just the beginning of the surprises.

FLYING TO NORTH MONGOLIA IN 1947 BIPLANE

There was no smoke pouring from the engines, no fire and no damage of any kind we could see. What's more, there was no airstrip, no buildings or any sign of habitation; and no pilots. Nothing. It's a strange phenomenon on the open steppe that it appears completely flat but is actually full of rises and dips, so a person can disappear in less than a hundred metres. The pilots had clearly headed off and disappeared in some direction. What should we do? We sat and waited for an hour ...... nothing. A couple of members of our group were keen to set off and try to find someone; but I felt it was safer to stay with the plane as, sooner or later, someone would miss the plane and come looking for it.

Another hour passed when suddenly the pilots reappeared laughing, carrying large milk cans calling out "Yowtsgai!" ("Let's go!" in Mongolian). As they jumped aboard the plane, the smell made everything fall into place. Airak! Fermented mare's milk. It was the Airak season. They must have spotted a herding family with a large string of horses and decided to land nearby. They had been drinking for the last two hours and brought back a supply for the remainder of the trip. What a choice: to stay here in the middle of nowhere, or get aboard with a couple of half-cut pilots. Deciding to press on, we reluctantly got aboard.

Lisa and I wiggled our way forward to keep an eye on the pilots As we flew further north, we saw the mountains begin to rise; and soon they were higher than we were. We called out to the pilots to fly higher, but they told us we couldn't go over. We had to go through; which seemed a really bad idea in a fragile canvas plane. Don't worry; we would fly up the valleys between the peaks, they told us confidently. This was fine, until the clouds began to close in. The pilots began to point in different directions and shake their heads with worried frowns on their faces. We began to pray in earnest: Lord, we need a way forward. If you don't open a way, this trip is going to be significantly shorter than expected. We came closer and closer to the peaks and the pilots began to debate whether it was possible to turn around in such a narrow valley. All of a sudden, the clouds parted, and a beam of sunshine pointed the way. It was such a relief as we squeezed between the peaks and saw the silvery reflection of the white lake ahead.

Over the next week, we worked from dawn until dusk fixing up the hut and getting our colleague set up. It was hard work due to the extreme cold, and at one point, while clinging to the icy roof attaching a solar panel, I learnt the hard way what happens when you hold frozen nails in your mouth and try to rip them free… blood everywhere!

It was a tough week but a good one. The local people were obviously overjoyed to have us there and excited about the education programme which our colleague would be starting. All was going well until the day she tearfully sat us down to tell us she couldn't stay. I couldn't believe it. After all the effort to get here and get set up. What was going on?

The reality of the call was hitting home for her. Stripped of the glamour and excitement, she was faced with the stark realisation as our leader feared, that she was not quite ready for this challenge. The Lord still had work to do in helping her to die to self and build the necessary faith and trust that God truly had her in His hands. We tried to get her to stay at least a month; but it wasn't to be, and we packed up and took her back. Sadly, when we got back to the city, she left Mongolia altogether and returned home.

For those who have never been faced with the harsh, terrifying reality of living in a wooden shack, with no electricity or running water, surrounded by people who don't speak your language or understand your culture; with unbelievably cold winter temperatures as low as -50°C; knowing you would be cut off from any assistance for part of each year until the snow in the mountain passes melted in spring, or the lake froze hard enough to travel on in winter, it would be easy, from the comfort of home, to sit in judgement on this sister and her desire to help those the world had passed by. If this is you, then I encourage you - try it. Then maybe you'll have earned the right to judge. One thing I do know for sure is: don't try it until God has fully prepared you. There are simply no shortcuts in allowing God to prepare us at each stage of our journey. If we try to rush the process, we risk losing it all.

God prepares us in His perfect timing to be ready for each stage of the journey. I know it can be frustrating and difficult waiting for God's perfect timing, but the waiting and trusting is a critical part of building the faith we need to carry us forward. We need to be prepared to ask God "What are you trying to teach me and what needs to change in my life so I am ready?" We need to have a right attitude and be open to learning and changing, to resist the temptation to go around frustrated, or impatiently demand that God work according to our timeframe rather than His. Successful ministry is revealed in God's time, neither grasped for, nor forced.

I remember our Bible college principal, a very wise and gifted teacher, saying "Hold on to ministry like a bird. Not so carelessly you drop it; but not so tightly you kill it". Even after allowing God to do His work of preparation, answering the call of God is often still a step of faith.

We had felt for some time that God was calling us to Mongolia, and in 1993 I got the opportunity to visit Mongolia briefly to 'spy out the land', as it were. We were on a short-term mission trip to Hong Kong and we met the leader of one of the Christian agencies working in Mongolia. She was in Hong Kong on furlough and invited me to stay in her apartment, for a short visit. It seemed too good an opportunity to pass up, and so I set off with no idea what I was in for.

I reached Beijing with no problems. There I bought a whole bunch of vegetables: cauliflowers, broccoli, beans etc., and stuffed them into my carryon bags to give to missionary families, as I'd been told you couldn't buy vegetables in Mongolia in winter.

Checking in for my flight to Mongolia, I found the ticket counter was overflowing with what I later learnt were Mongolian merchants bringing 'pigs' to Mongolia. A 'pig' was a duffel bag stuffed full of goods to sell and taped up with brown box tape so it resembled a stuffed pig: hence the name. At this time, after the withdrawal of Soviet forces and the declaration of a free democratic Mongolian state, the country was going through a period of economic collapse. Shelves in shops were bare; buying food and necessary goods was a daily struggle. So enterprising young Mongolian merchants were flying back and forth to Beijing, bringing back much-needed supplies.

When I finally got to the counter and handed over my backpack to check in, the airline guy asked if there was anything else I would like to pay? Being a fairly inexperienced traveller, I was confused, and said I didn't think there was anything else I needed to pay. He shrugged his shoulders and sent my bag through.

I boarded the plane and found my seat, only to discover there was only half of a seatbelt. I've never been convinced that a seatbelt would make much difference if the plane decided to plummet to the ground but it felt uncomfortable without one, so I looked around the crowded plane, spotted a spare seat and quickly sat down. I grabbed the seatbelt, glad to see there were the necessary two halves, only to discover the end attachment for one was missing. Huh; now what? Out of options, I tied the two halves together in my best reef knot and hoped I wouldn't need to test whether or not it would hold. What's more, it became clear why that seat was vacant, as the very large, very drunk Russian next to me hauled out a very large bottle of vodka and leaned across to me to begin a conversation monologue. The fact I couldn't understand a word of Russian totally escaped him, and for the entire flight I was bathed in copious amounts of second-hand vodka fumes.

Arriving at the airfield in Mongolia's capital Ulaanbaatar, I saw a truck pull up and began to dump luggage from our flight on the tarmac. 'Pigs' were disappearing left and right, and soon there were only a few confused foreigners left. It didn't take us long to work out that none of us had paid the 'extra payment' (otherwise known as a bribe) to have our bags actually loaded on the plane with us. What was worse was, foolishly I had packed all my warm gear in my checked backpack so I could fill my carry-on with vegetables. So there I was, standing on the tarmac at -30°c with nothing but... vegetables!

I managed to find the guide whom we'd arranged from Hong Kong to look after me for the week. He dropped me to the apartment. As I opened the door to the apartment, the lights went out and there was a power cut, which lasted all night. After knocking over a few items trying to feel my way around the freezing apartment in the dark, I wrapped myself in a carpet, closed my eyes, and thought "Welcome to Mongolia!"

Eventually I was reunited with my backpack and warm gear, and was able to move around delivering my vegetables to the few missionary families in the city. It's the only time I've seen people burst into tears at the sight of a cauliflower or piece of broccoli. I heard story after story of food shortages, of a bread ration that always seemed to run out just before it was your turn, and of power cuts that could last days and of the fear of what would happen if the city's steam heating system failed permanently. Walking along past the frozen, drab Soviet-style apartments, I saw shop after shop with completely empty shelves. I remember seeing a sheep's skeletal remains and thinking "how could anyone or anything survive here?"

One morning my young guide asked me if I wanted to visit a traditional herding family living in the countryside in a ger (a Mongolian felt tent). Absolutely! Who wouldn't want to experience such a thing? I was excited. Finally, I was heading for something that would inspire me about coming here.

We headed out across the steppe in an old black car that looked like it was from the 1950's. On the way he began to explain about the do's and don'ts of Mongolian traditional culture. Don't step on the wooden door frame when you enter. Go to the left-hand side and wait to be seated. Don't receive food or drink with the left hand, only the right and place your left hand under the elbow of the right arm to be polite; and especially if greeted by an older person.

Eat or drink whatever your given

But most of all- whatever you are given to eat or drink, you must eat or drink it, because to refuse their hospitality would be very insulting to people who were giving you their best. I wasn't sure I'd got it all but at least the last piece stuck with me. I must eat or drink whatever.

We entered the ger and sat down. So far so good. I was then given an enormous bowl of a milky liquid that smelled like a cross between vinegar and stomach bile. My guide explained to me this was Airak, a Mongolian delicacy. It was horse's milk which had been fermenting inside a skin container made from a sheep's stomach for the last three months.

Wow! That sounded intense; but I remembered what my guide had said about eating and drinking. So I lifted the huge bowl and began to chug it down, determined not to offend my hosts. One third into the bowl my stomach began to rebel and heave, two thirds in and I was fully in a cold sweat. I carefully placed the empty bowl on the table in the middle of the ger with teeth clenched desperately trying not to throw it all back up. In his list of do's and don'ts, my guide hadn't specifically talked about throwing up in the middle of a ger being culturally inappropriate, but I was guessing it wasn't the thing to do.

It was at that moment my guide learned across to me and said, "You shouldn't really have done that". What do you mean? I shouldn't have done what? "You shouldn't have drunk the Airak" he said in a worried tone. But what about the eat and drink thing?

Looking at me sitting in a cold sweat with my stomach heaving, he told me that foreigners usually get sick, even after drinking a small amount; and that the family were not happy that I drank it. But hang on: the whole reason for drinking it down was to not offend the family. What was going on? Then he explained… that was the entire winter supply for the whole family I had just drunk. Apparently, I was just supposed to take a small sip and pass it to the next person. Ooops! Someone could be in the doghouse!

He was right about one thing. By 10pm that night. I was as sick as a dog. By midnight I could hardly stand, and I knew I was in serious trouble. I remembered being told there was an American nurse staying in an apartment one floor below me. So I staggered down the stairs and I remember pushing on her door bell before blacking out. Later she told me she thought it was just a drunk at the wrong apartment; but felt she should check it out anyway. Catching sight of my blond hair through the peephole she realised it was a foreigner in trouble and took me in.

What an angel. God bless her. For the next two weeks she cared for me as I made a complete mess of her tiny apartment. I don't think there was an inch of that apartment I didn't throw up on. And the diarrhoea! There were so many times I had liquid explosively exiting my body top and bottom simultaneously! I remember sitting in her tiny toilet and vomiting so hard that it hit the bowl and splattered all over her walls. As I said: she was an angel.

I finally recovered enough to try to make the trip back to Hong Kong. Miraculously, I made it as far as my hotel room toilet in Beijing before having further bouts of violent vomiting. As I sat on the floor, stomach violently cramping and with my head in the toilet, I was calling out "God help me!" and thinking I will never, ever, ever, ever set foot in that country again. If all the Mongolian people don't get to hear the gospel and end up going to hell that would be a real tragedy, but I cannot go back there again. Certainly, I can't take a family there. Who can survive such a place?

It was that moment that the presence of God came on me and, in my mind, I saw a picture of the hands of Jesus holding a silver bowl with a dark red liquid and heard him say "Will you drink this cup with Me?" "Jesus no! No way! It's bitter, it's terrible!" I thought. "I know it's bitter," He said but "will you drink this cup with Me?"

At that moment I knew, because I knew, deep down inside He was calling us to Mongolia. The only question was: would I have the faith to answer the call? If this was the purpose I was created for, would I turn away from it, return to a normal, comfortable life in New Zealand and settle for God's second best for my life; or would I push past my fears and in faith say "Yes Lord, here I am send me". As I lay down my life and said yes in that little Beijing toilet, a twenty-year international ministry was born.

I'll never forget the concern and worry I felt when Alex was not on the plane as planned; communication with Mongolia was very difficult at this time. I didn't know what had happened, nor when he would be coming. When he finally arrived about two weeks later, he looked sick and so thin, he couldn't even have me hug him from the pain of all the vomiting. I could see something was heavy on his heart; we agreed at that time not to talk about what he felt God had spoken to him until I had prayed about our future. It was close to Easter at this time: I spent time reading and praying, then on Easter Sunday I felt the Lord say "Will you surrender your desires and go where I am leading you?" There was a sense of excitement and dread all at the same time. I knew very little about Mongolia at this point, except for some of the things Alex had shared. But the question still remained: will you trust me? Do you have the faith to step out beyond your comfort zone? The answer was "YES"!

CHAPTER 3

Faith for God's Provision

In the journey of faith there are several simple truths. One truth is that God provides for the journey. He doesn't call us to take a step and then not provide what we need to take the step. It may sound logical when we describe it like this, but it can be a real challenge to have the faith to put this into practice.

When looking back over our journey, we can see that this was a truth God wanted us to grasp right from the beginning.

> *When we knew it was right to step out and go on the mission trip to the Philippines and to Hong Kong, we priced our tickets, accommodation and food. It was going to cost us around $5,200. Right from the beginning we felt the sense that God was asking us to fully trust Him for the finances.*
>
> *We knew we had to start planning, but we also knew we could only afford to make this trip if God provided. We were excited and nervous about how this would all come together. We knew we had to do our part and be diligent in our saving. We had worked out that if we faithfully put away money for eleven months, we would have close to the amount that we needed. But... have you ever noticed that when you need to put money away, all of a sudden everything you own breaks down and somehow one ends up with bills that were*

never planned for. No matter how hard we tried, after four months the total amount we were able to save was a big fat zero.

I couldn't help my frustration with God, saying to Him… "Wait a minute, God; we feel this is Your leading. Surely You will provide?"

After seven months had passed, we had gathered up $300… there was not a chance this amount would work. I said to God, "This can't be right; what are You doing? We thought we heard You, but where's the money?"

Then my dad contacted us to say "This is crazy, going without money. I can lend you the money and then you can pay it back later." I have to say it was very tempting, naturally speaking, but in our spirit we felt that somehow God had a plan.

We declined dad's offer, and told him that we believed God was going to provide. Alex and I agreed in prayer… "We're putting our faith in You, God, and we are going to see how You will provide."

Although we were putting on a brave face, inside we felt sick. The doubts had started to really mess with our heads. Then later that day, we got a call from our church to say someone had dropped an envelope off for us. To our surprise there was money in it. Wow! Amazing! God, maybe You are in this. Then over the next few weeks we kept finding money in envelopes stuffed through our letterbox, hundreds of dollars at a time. The church was calling us every other day to say more and more envelopes were being delivered; and the money began pouring in.

When we counted the money, $3,000 had been donated and we were overwhelmed by the faithfulness of God. With less than two months to go, we waited expectantly to see where on earth the remaining $2,200 would come from.

Then one night, Alex had a dream; he was sitting at a well holding a cup and someone was taking water from the well and pouring water into the cup. He then shared the water with the Asian adults and children. Not fully understanding the dream, we held it close to our hearts.

Alex needed to have some physio on his leg, and during his visits to the physiotherapist, God began to open up a deeper conversation than just around the state of his leg. What came to light was that the physiotherapist had just become a new believer and had many questions on his mind, including a question about a dream.

He asked Alex... "How do you know if a dream is from God?" Alex responded, "Can you share some of the dream with me?"

The physiotherapist shared... "I was at a well taking water from it. I then poured the water into a cup that someone was holding."

Can you imagine what was going through Alex's mind at that moment?

As they talked it was clear that the two dreams somehow fitted together: it was the physiotherapist drawing the water from the well and Alex holding the cup. Then when Alex shared with him that we were about to go on a mission trip to Asia, the physiotherapist was beside himself with excitement, knowing his dream had been from God.

The physio sessions ended, and the physiotherapist had requested that Alex come and see him for one last time. Our thinking was... this is the bill being presented to us; after all it was in an envelope.

When we got back to the car, we took a big deep breath and opened it. Instead of finding a bill, there was $1,500 with a note stating... "Consider this water from the well".

Who would have believed God's provision would come this way? We had decided at the beginning that we wouldn't ask people for money or tell them how much we still needed. Alex had not discussed the trip with the physiotherapist, nor asked for any contribution. Instead, God had selected a man, a new believer, and had given him a dream so he could be part of God's provision for the trip.

We arrived at our departure date and even though our budget was still $200 short, we just knew God was showing so many signs, that it would be wrong for us not to step on the plane. Just as we were boarding, our phone rang. The dog that we had up for sale for several months had been sold. The money was being sent into our bank – the grand total of $200.

Saying we trust God to provide in many ways is easy, but then watching how God works it out can be a whole other story.

When we are believing God for that miracle always remember… Isaiah 55:8 'For my thoughts are not your thoughts, neither are your ways my ways; declares the Lord.'

God will look after even the small things

This was the beginning of a pattern of God providing for each stage of our journey as we took a leap of faith. We went without a salary, not knowing each month how much money God would bring into our bank account.

On our way to start our life in Mongolia, we had to spend a few days in Hong Kong for orientation with the organisation we would be working with. Feeling absolutely shattered, we arrived thinking we were at our accommodation; only to find the taxi could not take us up the hill to the apartment. We weren't even exactly sure where we needed to go. It was after 11pm and raining and was very muggy. The taxi driver said, "You get out here". We tried to explain that we couldn't carry all our bags, but he motioned for us to get out.

Fortunately, in Hong Kong there are many overhead rail tracks, so with 13 or so pieces of luggage, we stood under the tracks trying to keep dry until the worst of the downpour stopped. We made trips backwards and forwards until we finally had everything at the apartment. Drying out, we hit the sack totally exhausted.

The next morning we were going through our bags and that's when I discovered my little backpack wasn't there. Feeling absolutely gutted, I crumbled into a quivering mess. You might be thinking - it's just a backpack what's the big deal?

This was the start of our long-term work overseas. We had just left all our family and friends in New Zealand to embark on the call that we felt God was leading us into. That backpack had all my memories and treasures, the things that I felt would help me to make a home in Mongolia. It had my photos, the one thing that I treasured most of all; the cards and notes that people had written to us at our farewell; my precious book that friends had written in; my bible which I'd had since I was 16 years old, with all my little notes to self, written in the margins; and my Walkman (a handheld recorder that I would be able to tell our story on over the next few years).

Also, there was $100 cash, although I really didn't care about the money.

I felt as if my life had been ripped away from me. Everything that was important to me was in that little backpack and now it was gone. How could this happen, God? We have given up everything to serve you; and at the start of the journey, my backpack gets lost.

I was angry, frustrated, upset and grumpy. The night before had been dark, and we were tired. Why hadn't you counted the bags properly, Alex? In my heart I was blaming Alex. Surely you should have been more responsible, you're the husband, the leader. I felt resentful: you knew how much this backpack meant to me; why weren't you more careful. He spoke up and said "Let's just pray and see what God will do." I found it hard to believe there was any way it could possibly be returned.

We went back down to where we had been dropped off, but there was no bag to be found and again it was pouring down with rain.

My stomach churned. I wanted and needed that backpack. It was the one thing I had that would remind me of home. I can't go to Mongolia without it. I remember praying to God, "If there is any way you can bring that backpack back to me, please… it means everything to me. My photos were what I wanted most. With very limited mail delivery in Mongolia, I had to have my photos. It was the one way I knew I would feel connected to family and friends.

We went back again to the road the next day, still no bag. On the third day, someone from Hosanna (the place we were staying) was coming to visit us and on their way, they found a backpack on the side of the road. They turned up at the apartment with my backpack. I couldn't believe my eyes.

It was bone dry; the $100 was missing, but everything else was in it. My bible, books and precious photos were all ok, without any water damage.

It had been left where we had exited the taxi and it had been raining hard for those three days. But somehow here it was. How was this possible? Only you, God, could have made this happen.

Three days later? Seriously. The first morning when we looked, I felt God might give me my backpack back; but if someone had told me three days later "your bag will be found on the side of the road with everything in it but the money", I wouldn't have believed them.

After this incident, I began to really understand that God can do anything. I already knew God had called us, but now there was a new sense of knowing that God would watch over us; that He would provide not just what we needed, but also at times when we really wanted things.

After this experience, I wrote in my diary the verse from Philippians 4:19 'And my God will supply every need according to the riches of His glory in Christ Jesus.' *And it's been a great reminder to me.*

Nothing prepares you for the real thing

These early experiences were so important, given what was to come. When we arrived in Mongolia, we found it was in a state of economic collapse. It had been a satellite state of the Soviet Union for seventy years, until the Mongolian people rose up in peaceful protest and declared their independence. While the establishment of an independent republic brought unprecedented freedom for the Mongolian people, it also brought a time of severe economic hardship as the newly independent state struggled to transition from a communist state with a centrally run economy, to a democratic state with a free market economy.

Food was so scarce that we had to have ration cards to receive a loaf of bread each day, and it seemed the bread always ran out just before it was our turn. Shops were completely empty; we would go from place to place searching for food. It would take us hours every day, but God always came through, providing what we needed to be able to stay and continue to serve Him.

'And God is able to bless you abundantly, so that in all things at all times, having all that you need, you will abound in every good work.'
2 Corinthians 9:8

Not only for us but also for those we ministered to.

We moved to the countryside where life was even more challenging. We were living in a log cabin with no electricity and no running water. There was very little food available, mainly meat with some rice and almost no vegetables. Our transportation was three horses that we struggled to keep alive in the long Mongolian winters which were typically -30 to -40°C We chopped wood daily to keep the fire going; but at night, if you left a cup of water on the bench, by morning it would be ice. Life was challenging, to say the least.

I remember waking up one morning to the sound of Lisa sobbing her heart out in the bed beside me. "My hot water bottle...... has frozen...... there's ice in it." she sobbed. In the night as she turned over it had touched up against the wall beside her and frozen solid. This was to be one of many "God, get me out of here, I can't cope" moments we both would go through at different times over the next two years.

Left: IN THE SNOW FIELDS OF MONGOLIA

Never in my wildest dreams did I think we would ever be living like this. Mongolia is an incredibly beautiful but extremely harsh place. The land of Mongolia is so vast, almost two thirds the size of Australia with only about 2.5 million people. It was incredible that you could drive for days and hardly see a single soul. Journeying across the land was a sight to behold in itself. It's so raw and so vast it seems to go on forever. The wide-open spaces were so different from the hills and forests of New Zealand.

We lived east of the capital of Ulaan Baatar in a small town called Khentii. It was only 400 kilometres away, but on a good day it would take approximately nine hours to travel there, or on a bad day up to 16 hours. The journey would often feel like it had no end. But eventually we would arrive, with many adventures along the way. Some of these included getting stuck in rivers; vehicles getting flooded; flat tyres; being caught in a snowstorm; oil lines freezing and having to thaw them with a candle flame; and getting lost, as there were no roads as such, and certainly no signs or directions anywhere to be seen.

The area was known as the birthplace of Chinggis Khaan. As far as you could see, its endless plains were flat in all directions: brown, dry and dusty with a crust of ice and snow drifts for six months of the year. This was definitely not what I had pictured when Alex spoke about moving to the countryside. The picture that had come to my mind was a scene with a beautiful farm somewhere like the farmland in New Zealand, green and lush with forest; running water, electricity and a fireplace to keep you snug and warm. The reality was far from it. Khentii was none of these things.

We moved to Khentii in June of 1996. There was very little food available at that time and no electricity for refrigeration for food. Mind you, in winter that wasn't really a problem with the temperatures being so cold; but in summer, we would suffer badly from eating rotten meat which had gone off in the heat. Bathing once a week was a luxury; if you were lucky. We had to use a big plastic footlocker and it took hours to boil the water on the fire... it was such a tedious task. We would strip down one after another in the freezing cold. Using the same water, we would soap up, rinse off and get dry as quickly as possible. Alex would hate it, because he got to go last and the water was always muddy and cold by the time he got in.

LISA MAKING US A HOME IN THE WILDERNESS OF THE MONGOLIAN STEPPE

Initially we moved to the countryside to support another experienced foreign family who had spent years learning the Mongolian language and studied how to do community development projects and church planting. In the short time they had been there, they had been very successful in starting several successful community development projects and were planning to start a small church, at the request of new Mongolian believers who were enjoying their newly-won right to religious freedom and had decided they wanted to follow Jesus.

The idea was that we would move out to support them and learn from them for a year before moving to a different location, once we had learnt the language and had a better idea of what we were doing. Unfortunately, things didn't go according to plan. His wife had been having some health issues. As soon as we arrived, they left for home for a furlough. Instead of returning after a couple of months, they were never able to return. This left us to run several development projects (which we didn't know how to do), lead a church (which we didn't know how to do) and survive in the Mongolian countryside (can I write this again… which we didn't know how to do). All with knowing only a few basic sentences in Mongolian. In the natural, it should never have worked; and it wouldn't have, except for the provision of God.

God provided in so many ways over the next two years. He provided us with the most amazing local people to journey with: co-workers and neighbours who helped us to learn the language and the skills we needed to survive countryside life. We were taught the Mongolian way to do everything, from cutting wood and banking a fire for the night, to managing horses, to even providing us with an ancient Mongolian grandmother, who loved us unconditionally and scolded us whenever she felt we needed it.

We were working among the poorest of the poor: families with fathers who were cripples and not able to find work; children and youth whose parents had both died of disease; families who struggled to survive the harsh unforgiving winters of cutting icy winds and freezing temperatures; families who lived in old gers (felt tents) without their own animals for food or the animal dung, which was used to keep the fires going for heating and cooking.

With winter temperatures so extreme, heating was critical for survival. Living in the middle of the Mongolian steppe, we were miles away from a forest where you could collect wood. If you didn't have animal dung, the only way to heat your home was to hire a truck and travel to the forests up north (which were about four days away) and collect your winter wood supply. This was an expensive exercise and made wood a precious commodity.

As we have said, food was also often scarce; but even in the summer, when it was more plentiful, they could only afford to eat one meal every two to three days. For those of us who have grown up in wealthy nations, it can be hard to understand what this kind of poverty is like.

In the beginning, we tried to be the ones to meet their needs. We couldn't live knowing we had wood for a fire every day and these families didn't, so we told them to come and take our wood. The wood pile began to disappear in no time at all and we knew it was impossible to replace the wood until after the winter. It was too cold in winter for a truck to travel up north to the forested areas and the wood was frozen hard like iron so you couldn't saw it and split it. So we finally had to stop giving it away. The need was more than we had the resources to meet.

It was not more than God has the resources to meet, though.

OUR WINTER SUPPLY OF WOOD

Eating the dog's food

The people in Khentii were so poor that it was hard to watch them struggle with poverty day in and day out. We met one family who really were one of the poorest families we had encountered. They lived in an old coal shed. The father was blind in one eye and was crippled, and they had six kids. They had no food, and only one bed in the small room in which they lived. They rarely bathed over the winter months, because of the extreme cold. The kids barely had any warm clothes, and did not own warm shoes. Seeing them at those temperatures huddled around a candle to try and stay warm was hard to take.

One day the mother came over to our place with her son who was eleven years old. I was standing with my back to them and, when I turned around, I knew the young boy had taken something. The Mum said to him to put it back… it was a very awkward moment. He looked at me and said, "I am sorry; I was just hungry". As I looked around, I knew there had been no food put out, so I could not work out what he had taken. Then I realised the mouldy bread in the dog's bowl was gone; surely he hadn't picked this up?

Again his Mum told him to give it back; and from behind his back he pulled out the mouldy piece of bread that I had thrown into the dog's bowl. I was shocked and embarrassed, I said to him "No, please don't eat that. I can get you something else". He begged me, saying "Its ok I just need a little bit of the bread; I am so hungry. This will be enough for a few days". My heart sank. I explained to him that it was old bread for the dogs, not something people would eat. He begged me not to take it from him.

My heart ached for this family. So poor, the only way to survive was to beg and steal. They were not liked by many of the people in the town. I remember so clearly being at the market, seeing the Mum and giving her a hug and then the shopkeepers refusing to take my money as they now felt that I was dirty. How cruel and harsh people can be.

I have wondered to myself: "God, why is it that some have to go through life like this? To be born into such poverty… I realise how fortunate I am. But what is my responsibility in this? Do I even have responsibility for these people?"

Yes, we did share that there is a God who loves them dearly; but you simply can't just talk about God. People need to be met holistically: their spiritual, emotional, and physical needs are all important. We were able to provide the Mum with some work and teach her about trusting God. During this time she really learned to rely on God. I would see her go to the market and sit and pray, asking the Lord to provide. She would wait and see what God would do. So often someone would give her flour or some meat or bones. She had learned what it meant to trust God.

'And my God will meet all your needs according to the riches of his glory in Christ Jesus.' Philippians 4:19

When there's no doctor nearby

Even living in such difficult conditions with little medical support, God provided protection for our health. Although, as Lisa said, we suffered many bouts of food poisoning and I had an ongoing struggle with giardia, we toughened up and adjusted to the harsh life. God saved us from serious injury during the many falls from horses, vehicle accidents and so on.

Horse accidents could be serious, as Mongolian horses have two speeds: walk, and run flat out. I probably have to admit that some of my falls also had something to do with my love of racing my friends across the steppe. I remember one of my more spectacular falls happened when I was racing four friends at a flat-out gallop and my horse stepped in a jurrum hole[1]. Travelling at speed, the horse's foot suddenly sank into the hole and the horse fell forward, throwing me over its head. I know I did a couple of somersaults and somehow landed on my feet; and I think the horse did the same, because we both ended up standing eyeball to eyeball with each other, with no idea how we ended up on our feet and not on the ground with broken legs. Thank you, Jesus. In typical Mongol style, my friends then rode up clapping, whistling and shouting, "do it again, do it again, that was great, just like in the movies!" With vague thoughts about not putting the Lord your God to the test whirling around in my still spinning head, I decided to call it quits for that day.

There's nothing quite like living in a place without medical support to stretch your faith. In the developed world we are so used to having a medical safety net for whenever anything goes wrong that it's actually hard to wrap your head around what life is like when it's not there.

I will never forget the first time we saw a serious accident in Mongolia. We were working in a town called Muruun in the north of Mongolia. It was mid-winter and, as usual, a freezing wind was blowing, carrying ice crystals. Even though we were bundled up in fur boots, sheepskin Dels (Mongolian robes), fur hats and gloves, the ice crystals seemed to always find a bit of exposed flesh to sting. We were trudging head down through the snow when two guys on a motorbike came out of nowhere and raced by, zig-zagging like crazy. Like a moth to a flame, somehow they managed to head straight for the only obstacle in sight, a concrete pole. With a sickening CRUNCH they hit it head on, while still accelerating.

---

1. Jurrum: Are small mice like creatures that dig dozens of small burrows in an area so when a horse steps on the area it sinks up to its fetlock.

We ran as fast as we could, all bundled up in our winter gear. As we reached the bike, two things hit my mind. The first was the sharp fumes of leaking petrol and the tick-tick of hot metal, so we carefully dragged the two of them clear of the bike. The second was: the guy driving the bike had no scalp and his face was a mask of blood; or as I later discovered the scalp was peeled back and hanging off the back of his head.

As good first aiders we secured the site and then checked the passenger who was unconscious was still breathing and had a pulse. We examined them quickly to ensure neither were bleeding out from other injuries. We put the unconscious passenger in the recovery position and managed to stop the worst of the bleeding from the scalp.

So far, all of this was 'normal' to us, no different than if we had come upon a bike accident back in New Zealand. Okay; we had done our bit. Now it was time to hand over to the professionals. Then we suddenly remembered: there was no ambulance to call, actually no phone either. There were no emergency services. There was a town doctor, but he had gone away further out into the countryside to visit a remote herding family and no one knew whether he would be back this week or next week or next month. There was no one. With a sick feeling in my stomach, I realised we were responsible.

It was a surreal moment as we knelt beside them in the snow. God what do we do? We're not doctors. But there was no one else in sight. I gave them both a more thorough examination and as I did so, the passenger came around and started to groan. It was clear he had some sort of internal injuries. Both were rapidly going into shock. The sun would soon be going down, and the temperature would drop to below -40°C.

First Aid 101 had taught us the risk of moving people with internal injuries, but it was clear that neither would survive much longer in the freezing conditions. It seemed to take forever to get them to the nearest ger, with the passenger groaning and crying out in pain as we carried him. All I could think about was "Oh God, we're killing him…" but eventually we managed to get them to shelter with a warm fire.

While the fire ensured they wouldn't die of hypothermia, it caused another problem, as the driver's head defrosted and began to bleed everywhere. Clearly the scalp needed to be sewn back on. There was no surgical needle or sutures but the mother of the ger where we were sheltering had a normal needle and thread. After doing the best I could to disinfect the skull, I set to working stitching the top of the guy's head back on. I admit it did look a bit Frankenstein-ish with these big black stitches across his forehead and around the sides of his head and I don't think I have a future as a plastic surgeon; but it did stop the bleeding.

This began a process of us looking after the two of them until the doctor returned the following week. Living in a developed nation, it's amazing how much we totally take for granted the safety net of professional emergency services. This was one of many experiences where we witnessed the suffering of people around the world who don't have access to adequate medical care.

I can't remember if it was before or after this motorbike incident that we were delivering medical aid to a remote location in the far north of Mongolia. We had been given a truckload of ex-military supplies and equipment. Unlike some of the donated medical stuff, which is often useless in developing contexts, this load was great because it was high quality, really suitable for the basic medical care countryside doctors could provide.

We stopped at a very remote small town which had once had a functioning medical centre. I met with the doctor and we talked about what was needed for him to begin to operate the centre again and what he was capable of providing. As the medical supplies were so scarce, we wanted to ensure we only gave him what he could use. I asked him if he had broken equipment which we might be able to arrange to be repaired back in the city. He laughed and showed me his only piece of equipment in the whole medical centre… An old 1930's typewriter. "Listen," he said. "Can you hear the key strike the paper? Yes? Then you're not deaf!" As you can tell he was quite a hard case. We had a long debate about whether we should give him surgical equipment or not. He assured me he was by far the best surgeon in Mongolia and could do surgery if we left him the surgical tools, needles, sutures etc. "But you have no anaesthetic", I argued. "Not a problem for me" he assured me.

As we boarded our truck to head further north, I remember saying to Lisa it was probably a waste leaving the surgical gear with him. It would probably end up back in the city sold on the black market; but heck, I liked the guy and his can-do attitude.

As it turned out, we returned about a week later on our way back south and were met with a huge round of hugs and slaps on the back. The doc was beside himself with excitement. Shortly after we departed, a herdsman came to the clinic with acute appendicitis. Normally the man would just have died but the doc had operated using our surgical tools and he was alive. He grabbed me by the hand, and we rushed into the centre to see that, sure enough, they had a bed set up. There lying in the bed was a man with his midsection wrapped in bandages and a huge grin on his face.

It was about then I remembered about the lack of anaesthetic and asked the doc how could he do such an operation without anaesthetic? He laughed loudly and replied "It wasn't a problem. We don't have anaesthetic, but we do have plenty of vodka!" Yes, he'd had the man drink half a bottle of vodka before cutting him open and taking out his appendix. I did wonder whether the other half was needed by the surgeon, but I decided not to ask. I asked the patient how he felt about the whole ordeal. He told me it was strange feeling the doc's hands working around inside of him; but his only complaint was that he thought the brand of vodka wasn't the best. For such a procedure, he felt they should use only the good stuff. Needless to say, he was very grateful to be alive.

Not all stories have such a happy ending. I remember the feeling of shock and sadness when my team of doctors in Nepal told me they needed to amputate the right arm of a nine-year-old boy and asked if it was okay to go ahead.

Working amongst insurgencies…

During the civil war in Nepal, I had managed to negotiate with both the Government military and Maoist guerrilla forces to be able to lead teams of doctors and nurses into remote mountainous areas where there had been no access to medical services for years, because the educated, professional people including the doctors had fled the area. We would go to a remote area and hold a medical camp for a week. My overworked doctors would work nonstop, seeing hundreds of patients before moving to the next location.

To return to this poor boy. What made it so horrific was this all happened because weeks before he had gotten a scratch on his arm. Without any access to disinfectant, it had become septic and turned into gangrene. The boy lost his arm because he didn't have access to what for us would be a short trip to the supermarket or chemist for a $5 bottle of disinfectant. Unbelievable!

Is it any wonder we hear so often of God doing miraculous wonders of healing in third world countries? For so many, turning in faith to God for healing is not a choice of "should I go to the doctor" or "should I pray for my healing?" Healing is the only option.

LISA ASSISTING WITH A NUTRITION SURVEY

At times in our journey, it seemed like we were going from one crisis situation to another. Each crisis would have its own demands and needs that we never had the power, influence or resources to resolve. At each crisis we had to learn to reach a new level of faith in God's provision.

In Mongolia it was the poverty; but in Nepal it was security. You never knew when or where violence would erupt. Travelling in the midst of an insurgency, or what was in effect a civil war, was challenging. You never knew what to expect.

By the grace of God, I had also been able to negotiate successfully with the Nepali Government, Nepali Army, the Maoist guerrillas and the United Nations, and was able to transport and distribute food to remote villages where children and villagers were starving. Getting this agreement had been a miracle. It had taken months of building relationships and trust with all parties at a time when everyone was suspicious of everyone else. To be caught meeting with a Maoist Commander meant at best, deportation, and at worst, imprisonment.

To arrange such a meeting was difficult and dangerous. You had to travel to remote locations ensuring you were not being watched, then use various ways to arrange meetings; such as walking along a certain trail to a certain tea shop and asking if a certain Mr Thapa was in. You would be told a time to come back and when you returned you would be told if he was going to be in or not. In other words, whether he had agreed to meet with you or not. If he did agree, you would be taken to an even more remote location for the meeting. It was dangerous because on one side, the Nepali Army was constantly hunting for the Maoist leaders; and on the other side, if a meeting was compromised, you could be accused by the Maoists of selling them out.

Finally, everyone was on board with allowing us to go ahead. Then the really hard work started, transporting tons of food over some of the most mountainous terrain in the world, between Nepali Army-controlled areas and into Maoist-controlled areas. It proved impossible to do by land; we had to fly the food up into the mountains by plane or helicopter before carrying it by donkeys or porters out to the distribution locations.

In one location in Kalikot, the small town was built clinging to a sharp ridgeline, so there was no airstrip; only a helicopter landing pad. The wind was always blowing and as you came in, the wind-shear would toss the helicopter around like a toy. The ancient Russian pilot looked at least ninety, but I guess was only in his sixties or seventies (he'd been old when he flew for the USSR in the invasion of Afghanistan). It always amazed me how well he flew his equally ancient Russian helicopter. Every time he managed to circle once and then plummet straight down to land on this tiny landing pad, with the ground falling steeply away to the front and rear. It was an area only a few meters larger than the helicopter itself and was like landing on the head of a pin.

The terrain was only part of the challenge, though. Once the Nepali Army started using civilian helicopter to transport troops, the Maoists would shoot at the helicopter from the mountain tops as we flew by.

A TRANSPORT HELICOPTER DESTROYED BY MAOIST GUERRILLAS

I remember arriving one afternoon at the airport where we would load up the food for the flight north into the mountains, and seeing the pilot scooping what looked like red paint out of the cockpit on the co-pilots side. I remember thinking: "Why would anyone be carrying red paint in the cockpit?" As I got closer, the copper tang of fresh blood hit me, and I realised it was blood, a lot of blood being scooped out. In his broken English, the pilot told me how his co-pilot had been shot and killed on the morning run by Maoist ground fire. I wasn't sure how good his heart was. Realising what a shock it must have been for him, I asked him if he wanted to call it a day and try again tomorrow; but after a couple of long pulls from his large vodka bottle, he declared he was good to go. He was an amazing old guy, hard as nails. So off we went.

I remember more than one drama, we met while flying in a small cargo plane up to the mountainous North West, bringing rice for distribution to some of the worst-affected villagers. The planes we used were small twin-engine with two clamshell doors at the back that opened to allow a pallet of sacks of rice to be loaded from the rear. A cargo net would be thrown over it, and we would usually lie on top of the cargo net.

On one trip I was travelling up with my Nepali friend and colleague who had shared so many of my adventures in Nepal with me. Soon after take-off, the rear doors began to rattle in a strange way. At first we ignored it; but it kept getting louder and louder. As we began to check it out, all of a sudden, the doors burst open and started flapping behind us.

Wind was whipping around us and we lay there clutching the cargo net, holding on as if our lives depended on it (err... actually, they did!). That was all good; until we felt the pallet give a lurch towards the open doorway and then another one. I had this sick feeling in the pit of my stomach as I looked around frantically for something to brace the pallet and stop it falling out the back with us clinging to it; but there was nothing.

We braced our legs in desperation against the struts on the side of the plane and tried to hold the pallet; but it just kept on lurching to the rear, determined to do a kamikaze out the back and take us with it. It was right at this moment my friend yelled across to me "Just like Indiana Jones!" referring to a scene from one of the Indiana Jones films. For some reason it seemed like the funniest joke in the world and we laughed ourselves stupid. I still don't know why it was so funny.

I guess it had something to do with the fact that after all we had been through in the conflict together here, we were about to be killed by a faulty door and a contrary cargo net that would not stay in the plane.

You could call it coincidence, but I know that is when God once again intervened with His provision of divine protection because it was at the moment, when it seemed nothing was going to stop us being ejected out the back, that the plane's nose dropped; and we began to descend to the airstrip. With the nose now pointing downward, the pallet and cargo net dutifully retreated back inside the plane and we landed safely.

Another time doing that same run, we had flown from the flat southern terrain up through the valleys between the towering peaks. The plane finally climbed to the Jumla valley and we were on final approach to the tiny airstrip when, out of nowhere, clouds poured into the valley, completely covering the airstrip. The pilot circled a couple of times before telling me he couldn't land. We had to return and try again in a couple of days.

I remember feeling so frustrated as I sat that night being eaten alive by the hungriest mosquitos I'd ever seen. All that work to get the rice and the plane and arrange the distribution and now it was all going down the drain, all because of some cloud that decided to come out of nowhere. Seriously, does God not know what we are trying to do?

It was about that time my satellite phone rang. It was from my team in Jumla. I could hear gunfire and the odd explosion in the background. Yes, the team were all safe and sheltering in our hut; but they were worried about me. Why me? I was safe miles from the fighting.

What I didn't know was that my plane had been descending to land at the exact time the Maoist attack hit the airstrip. As the shooting started, they had watched my plane veer off and disappear into the clouds and didn't know if we had been hit or whether we had been able to land safely. We knew nothing about all this happening on the ground ...... but God did.

JUMLA AIRSTRIP: THE SCENE OF SPORADIC FIGHTING

Why don't I believe it was all coincidence? Because when these kinds of things happen again and again after a while you realise there is no way this is all just coincidence. Coincidence is random and occasional. What we experienced was the constant and deliberate intervention of our loving Heavenly Father.

Finding courage in the midst of fear

When we lived in Nepal, I was pretty much confined to Kathmandu. I wasn't excited when we moved there anyway; and to be living there during a time of turmoil was not my idea of enjoying life. Many times we would hear bombs exploding. Some days and they would call "bandht days"; that's when there were strikes and they would close off roads. No travel was allowed; tyres and other things would be burning in the streets. It wasn't safe going out. Riots and protests would break out randomly.

One time, ten Nepalis had been beheaded while working in Iraq. There was an uproar within Kathmandu; thousands of people took to the streets. The Army put Kathmandu on lockdown. Alex called me from the office in the morning to say to get our daughter Monqtuya from school. He'd get home when he could.

They put on the news that everyone was to stay home. No one was allowed to leave their homes or the city. It was all over the news that shops were being broken into and fires were being started downtown. Things did not look good. Everything within me felt afraid; but my only thought at that point was that I needed to get my daughter from school. At that moment we received a text message from school saying they were on lockdown and the kids would remain within the school grounds.

My head was spinning. No-one knew how long this would go on for and I knew that the British school where she was could be targeted. I had to get my daughter. I called some other Mums and they wanted to get their kids as well.

Our house was situated on a road that had an army base at the end of it. I and about five other mums headed down towards the school. There were trucks driving around with loudspeakers ordering everyone to stay inside. Fear welled up within me as I approached the school and saw there were tanks across the road, with no way to get to the school.

As we approached, the soldiers pointed their weapons toward us and motioned for us to stop. Fear turned to anger: we began to run at the soldiers and tanks. Without any thought for what might have happened, we ran through the line of soldiers, climbed up and over the tanks, and entered the school to retrieve our kids. That overwhelming sense of relief when I held Monqtuya was intense.

The fear in that moment and choice to trust God wasn't easy, but you go with what your gut tells you. Many times in the countries we have worked in, I have felt Godly fear and anger well up within me.

One time when we were in Mongolia and Alex was away on a trip, Monqtuya and I were out. She was holding my hand, walking next to the stroller, when a guy grabbed my bag from the bottom of the stroller and took off. I hadn't fully realised what had happened as the street was very crowded when I suddenly heard someone yell in Mongolian that "he stole that white woman's bag".

Have you ever just reacted without fully thinking about what the consequences may be? Well; this was one of those moments. I let go of two-year-old Monqtuya's hand and took off after that guy.

The bag had my apartment keys and my address in it and it was the only key to our place. I knew if I didn't get it back he would have access to my apartment. As I caught up with him, I planted my knuckles into his back: he fell forward, throwing my bag away. I grabbed my bag and breathed a sigh of relief; only to suddenly realise I had left my daughter behind in a crowded street. Fear rose up within me as I realised I had run about 50 metres; and with the crowd of people between us, I couldn't see her.

I immediately prayed "God, let her still be there" as I ran back to where I'd left her. Thankfully, she was with a little old Mongolian grandmother who was holding her hand. I remember that moment feeling so overwhelmed; I began to cry as I realised what could have happened to her.

In this life there are so many times we can find ourselves afraid. Afraid of sickness, afraid our kids could be taken, afraid of being alone, afraid of death. How do we cope with fear? Choosing to trust God no matter what happens; yes, it's scary; yes, it feels uncertain; but God is worthy of our trust.

As we continued on our journey, we were tested in many areas of our faith from provision to protection; and so my faith continued to get stronger. Yet there was one thing I always said I would never really cope with, and that would be being caught in the sea and the thought of drowning.

Why do I share this? Well; on one holiday in Thailand, we were out on the sea in a long-tailed boat (a small open boat about nine metres long with an outboard engine) and this was exactly the position I found myself in. My parents had joined us for a week's holiday together and we were staying at a small island called Phi Phi Island. It was about 40 kilometres from the larger "party island" of Phuket, which was full of young party-goers partying hard all night, waking up face in the sand on the beaches the next morning.

The one thing Phuket had which we needed was an airport and flights to the mainland. We had a great week with my parents. My mother was going to stay a few more days, but my father had to return to New Zealand. We took a long-tailed boat to Phuket and dropped him at the airstrip before going down to the beach to find a long-tailed boat to return to Phi Phi Island.

Usually there would be half a dozen boat owners falling over themselves to take us, but this time no-one was interested. We started to get worried: it was getting late in the afternoon; we had nowhere to stay on Phuket.

(Can I jump in…? Just a hint for fellow travellers. When boatmen who are usually desperate to earn cash suddenly won't put to sea for even double the usual fare… it's time to stay on the beach! - Alex)

Finally, Alex managed to convince a boatman to take us. I was a bit worried his boat seemed to be in worse condition than the others; but it was late in the afternoon, and I was worried that we had nowhere to stay. Besides, the boatman was saying "We go… We go. NOW!"

Reluctantly, we all climbed on to the long-tailed boat and set off. Within about 15 mins, as we came around the point, I noticed that the swells were larger than they had been in the morning; but the sun was still shining, and the weather looked okay.

When we were about halfway across, it all started. The weather took a sudden turn for the worse. A billowing line of angry black clouds raced towards us and immediately we were being pounded by wind and rain. The wind was blowing so hard that the rain was coming at us horizontally, and stung like icy daggers. The waves got bigger and bigger; the tiny little Thai boatman was struggling to control the boat as wave after wave battered the long-tailed boat.

I really thought "This is it", and fear gripped me. The thought of dying was okay, I knew where I would go; but the thought of dying by drowning was way too much. I had such a fear of the sea and I was so angry at Alex. He had said it would be fine, that we weren't even going that far. Even my Mum had said she didn't think it was a good idea to go; but Alex had pushed us to get on the boat.

(Jumping in again… Second lesson… Sometimes mothers-in-law DO know what they're talking about! - Alex)

I was sure the boat was going to flip; I so clearly remember saying to Alex "If this boat flips and you lose Monqtuya (our daughter), I'll never forgive you". I was so terrified! Then it got worse. As we approached Phi Phi Island, the wind and waves were pushing us closer and closer to the rocks. All it would take is for the struggling engine to quit, and in minutes we would be piled up on the rocks.

I gripped the side of the boat holding on for dear life. I knew it had to do with the water; but wasn't I serving the same God who calmed the waves and wind? I was finding it hard to focus on anything let alone God, and Alex was not helping. He was singing some sea shanty as loud as he could and talking some rubbish about keeping up the morale of the crew. I felt angry and afraid. He loved boats; and even though he was telling me everything would be fine. I knew enough to know at any moment we could be swamped and go under.

With the noise of the wind, the rain and thunder and everything else, I just didn't care. I was just plain scared. I cried out to God and I began to sing. I can't even remember what I sang; but this overwhelming sense of peace flooded over me. I did however have to keep my eyes closed just to cope as the boat climbed up one side of the wave put! ..... put! .... put! .... put! then teetered right up on the top of the waves and then would come crashing down put! put! put! put! If you've seen that movie 'The Storm', when the boat goes up against the waves: that's how it felt. Even now I feel sick as I think about it.

Eventually, much to my surprise, we made it to shore, drenched, cold and shaken. We ran from the beach dodging flying rubbish, palm branches and chairs and made it inside the diving resort where we were staying. When we got there the staff asked us where we suddenly appeared from. When we explained we had been out on the water and just arrived from Phuket, they were horrified.

The next morning, we went out to the beach to see the damage from the storm. We were shocked to see so many massive palm trees ripped out from the ground and blown over. Windows, tables and chairs had been smashed. The storm had left quite an impact, but for me the impact was that from then on I knew without a doubt the only way you get through any type of serious storm is to find God's peace in the midst of it all. It didn't mean I wasn't scared, but finding peace allowed me to trust Him even though I was afraid.

Having faith in God's provision of protection was to become a lifestyle in the years following as our work and ministry increasingly focused on conflict areas. I'll relate a couple of examples of the work I was doing so you get the idea.

South Sudan – Apocalypse now

I did some work in the north of South Sudan along the border area between the government-controlled and opposition-controlled areas of the Nile River. You know you're in a high-risk zone when the UN plane touches down on the airstrip and is immediately surrounded by UN peacekeeping soldiers and you're rushed into a convoy of armoured vehicles and driven at speed to the UN firebase. The airstrip was continually changing hands between government and opposition militias. Only a couple of days before I arrived, the UN firebase had been attacked.

I was there to observe and report on an airdrop of food supplies which was to take place across the river in opposition-held territory. To get there, we had to leave the relative security of the UN firebase and drive through the town of Malakal to the river. The UN guys thought we were crazy.

Malakal had once been a thriving regional centre with its own industry and university. Now as we drove slowly through town, we witnessed a scene from some weird post-apocalypse zombie film. The town was a ghost town, abandoned by people fleeing for their lives. The buildings had been damaged in the fighting. Windows were broken and doors smashed in. There were burnt-out vehicles and other vehicles abandoned where they had run out of fuel. Everywhere the jungle was rapidly resurging. In the cracks in the road, in people's homes and the windows of the university, the new jungle grew, covering man's failed attempt to shape the land for a more prosperous future. From time to time we passed groups of militias hanging around smoking on street corners, watching us with suspicion and barely concealed hostility.

From there we boarded a small open launch and headed up the Nile River. The river marked the boundary. On our right we had government militia, on our left opposition militia. You could feel the eyes watching us over gunsights. All it would take was for one nervous guy with a finger on the trigger and we would be in the middle of a murderous crossfire with nowhere to go. About an hour later we arrived at the opposition outpost and again faced hostile stares from armed militia, many of whom were young. Our local team had done an amazing job of setting up for the food distribution in the most extreme conditions, and a day later we were on our way back to the UN firebase. Amazingly, in a region ruled by the power of the gun, a region of mass hunger, where all resources were scarce, we had managed to distribute tons of food into the hands of the people who really needed it.

CHILDREN HAPPY TO HAVE WATER AND FOOD IN THEIR BELLIES

I often felt like I was in a bubble of God's protection. Fighting, violence and killing would be happening all around me, but somehow not where I was at the time.

It was the same in Afghanistan. I needed to travel from Hirat to the neighbouring province of Badghis to look at the feasibility of starting some new community development projects. There were two ways to get there - by plane or by road. It was hard to get a seat on the UN flights, but our local security guys were not happy about my plans to travel by road. I've learnt to trust the instincts of local people, especially in conflict areas; and I just had a feeling the road was not a good option. Amazingly, at short notice, I was able to get on the UN flight.

I had a great week in a very remote part of Afghanistan, working with local villages to plan several key development projects to help them with water access. I was the only foreigner for hundreds of kilometres. I knew we were close to Taliban controlled territory, and I was very vulnerable.

Left: NEW VILLAGE WATER SUPPLY, AFGHANISTAN

At each village I was welcomed by the village elders and assured that, as their guest, I was under their protection. I was deeply moved by the Afghan people, their culture of hospitality, and what it meant to be a guest. They had so little but were always prepared to share what they had. They made it clear to me that they were responsible for the welfare of their families. They weren't looking for handouts, but they simply didn't have the resources to undertake the level of civil construction that a government would normally do. They were serious about their promise that should the Taliban fighters show up, they would fight to protect me.

The Afghan people, their resilience and determination to survive, despite the international conflict being fought on their land and their generous hospitality, made a huge impact on me. So much so that years later back in New Zealand, when an Afghan refugee family was having difficulties with some local gang members, I felt compelled to front up to the gang and give them a lecture on hospitality!

There were a few tense moments when a couple of times I was suddenly surrounded by shouting armed fighters leaping out of vehicles or waving us down on the road, but each time they turned out to be friendly and were just happy to see us.

I returned to Hirat, confident that we would be able to support the villages to make a significant improvement in their lives and grateful for the protection of the villagers; but even more so, for God's protection. This was especially true when, upon returning to our office in Hirat, I learned that at the same time I had been in the field, a group from a different INGO had tried to travel to Badghis by road. They hit an IED (improvised explosive device) and several foreigners were killed. I had dodged another one: thank you, God.

These are just some of the examples of ways in which God was faithful in providing protection for us on our journey. There are many other examples we know about and could talk about; and I'm sure there are many, many other times we don't know about, when God faithfully watched over us.

'The LORD is my rock, my fortress and my deliverer; my God is my rock, in whom I take refuge, my shield and the horn of my salvation, my stronghold.' Psalm 18:2

CHAPTER 4
ATM Faith Machine

With the arrival of the era of fake news, our last expectation that news media outlets and our political leaders were bound by a sense of professional pride or moral integrity to speak the truth, has been torn away. If indeed there was a time when the media and political leaders felt honour-bound to speak the truth and only the truth, that time is long gone.

Unfortunately, this trend is not confined to the media and political leaders. Increasingly we see the promotion of fake news or fake doctrine by prominent Christian leaders, backed by multimillion-dollar businesses that are promoting and selling a range of personal philosophies under the label of biblical truth.

Nowhere is this more evident than in the area of faith. Their typical fake faith message goes something like this. If you have faith you can name or claim anything you desire, be it full health, wealth and prosperity, or success; and God will give it to you.

God is presented as a heavenly ATM machine. You put your faith card in the machine and out pours the blessings in the denomination of your choice.

What I mean by this is that according to this type of faith, not only do we expect the blessings to flow, but we also expect to define how God blesses us. We expect God to use our definition of blessing, which is usually more riches, more material things, complete health with of course instant healing, and without doubt… the avoidance of any hardship and suffering.

But what happens if God doesn't give me the blessing that I prayed for or claimed?

They have a quick answer for this… Well, brother/sister; it's just you don't have enough faith. In other words… It's your fault. If you only had generated enough faith from the 'FAITH ATM MACHINE' you would receive what you asked for. It is all about you. All you need to do is buy another set of faith series of CD's, make a significant donation, never question the one who asks for the money and…. They'll help you generate the level of fake faith you need to get the blessing of your choice. After all… your money goes in… and… cha-ching, blessing comes out. Sound familiar?

For those of you who believe in the Fake Faith: have you ever considered, for I know those teachers will never point it out… Acts Chapter 3?

Peter and John are on their way to the temple (church of that day) and a lame man asks them for money. Their reply is that they don't have money… can you believe this? These guys are on way to church with no money for temple taxes (offering). Yet, with no offering from the lame man, no sales of Peter or John's CD's, not even a slight hint of faith from the lame man that he was believing for a healing. Peter declares… "Silver and gold I do not have, but what I do have I give to you. In the Name of Jesus Christ of Nazareth, walk!" No red tape, just God. Wow! Imagine what it would be like if you didn't have to pay to receive a blessing.

A Hebrew understanding of Faith

Fake faith? That's a pretty big claim, given there are some real heavy hitters in the Christian world promoting this type of faith. Kind of arrogant to challenge this, isn't it? Well: it would be if it was coming from me; so let's go to the ultimate authority, the Word of God, and not just quote one or two passages. Let's look at what is truly a biblical understanding of faith.

In this day and age there are many Bible translations. I am sure you know there is more than just the one you use. But are you aware that there were many more translations even before the one that you use? And some of these translations were translated from another translation; like the Chinese Whispers game: what started out correctly never finishes correctly.

I am a big believer that to understand anything in its wholeness, one must go to the foundation of it… in other words, the "why" for it? For this to happen with any Bible translation, we must go back to the original text, Hebrew.

The Hebrew word for 'Faith' is 'Emunah'. It is interesting to note that Emunah has a root meaning which is 'Aman'. The word Aman[2] means… to make firm, secured or supported.

It has the idea that faith is fixed to something or someone. It is not about the individual; it is directed towards someone or something. When applied to faith in God, it means a faith that is fixed on the person of who God is. It is not in what He does or doesn't do; and certainly not in the belief that I have the power to direct God.

The Bible again and again encourages us to have faith in who God is: to trust IN God. Passage after passage describes the blessings that

---
2. Strong's Hebrew Lexicon H539 "Aman"

flow from having the faith to trust IN God. I would encourage you to check out more scriptures, but here are just some…

'The LORD is my strength and my shield; my heart trusts IN him, and he helps me.' Psalm 28:7

'Trust IN the Lord forever, for the Lord, the Lord himself, is the rock eternal.' Isaiah 26:4

'When I am afraid, I put my trust IN you.' Psalm 56:3

'Many are the woes of the wicked, but the LORD's unfailing love surrounds the one who trusts IN him' Psalms 32:10

'It is better to take refuge IN the Lord than to trust in humans.' Psalm 118:8

'Commit your way to the Lord; trust IN him, and he will do this.' Psalm 37:5

'But blessed is the one who trusts IN the LORD, whose confidence is in him. Jeremiah 17:7

Real Faith – An anchor in the storms of life

A faith that is real, with substance that will sustain you through the tough times, must be attached to the person of God. A faith that is built upon your own ability to direct God will let you down when you need it most. It's a paper tiger, it's smoke with no substance to it.

I guess it's like an anchor on a ship. An anchor keeps a ship safe in a storm, only when it's firmly attached to the bottom. You can have a very fancy-looking anchor; but if it doesn't hold you to the bottom, it's no use.

This reminds me of a holiday we once had in Australia. While we were living and working internationally, we had many great holidays with many great memories. One holiday I'd rather forget was the one when my mother kindly arranged for us to spend a week together in a houseboat, cruising lazily up a river in Queensland Australia.

It sounded like the perfect restful and relaxing holiday. We would rent a houseboat and slowly meander our way up this beautiful river, stopping each night at a new location. Maybe catch some fish and catch a few rays of sunshine. It all sounded great. So we picked up the houseboat, and we were all excited to set off on this relaxing houseboat holiday.

Unfortunately, by halfway through the first day, the weather started to turn nasty. Dark clouds rolled in, the wind began to rise, and the waves began to build. We decided to stop early and look for a safe place to anchor up and spend the night. Eventually we found what we thought was a reasonably sheltered area on the bend of the river.

When we had taken the houseboat from the owner that morning, we had checked to make sure we had everything we needed. I knew we would be anchoring each night at a new location, so I made sure to check out the anchor rig. It was a nice shiny new anchor with plenty of anchor chain and I thought that with a good solid anchor, we should have no trouble anchoring at night.

So now it was time to put the anchor to the test. I put it over the side and made sure we had plenty of line out so it would set properly. The wind continued to rise, and the waves grew larger, until a full gale was blowing. My mother, being an old sailor from way back, had taken some markers so that we would know if the anchor was holding true and I remember the moment when we looked at each other and both of us realised our anchor was not holding. In fact, we had started to drift quite rapidly across the river toward some rocks on the other bank.

There was nothing for it but to start the engine, raise the anchor and move again across the river and reset the anchor. We did this, only to find that once again, the anchor wasn't holding, and we were drifting rapidly across the river. A houseboat is something like a large biscuit tin floating on top of the water, with very large sides. The wind easily catches these sides and blows the boat around, making it extremely difficult to manoeuvre the boat and for the anchor to hold. By now it was dark, and rain was pouring down, so visibility was only a few metres. With the wind continuing to blow stronger and stronger and no visibility, we couldn't safely move to another section of the river. We spent an entire night setting the anchor, drifting across the river, raising the anchor, moving back across the river, then resetting the anchor.

The next morning when it became light, we managed to navigate our way back down the river and with great difficulty, return the houseboat to its dock. We climbed back into our car, soaking wet, frozen and absolutely exhausted. It was the opposite of the relaxing holiday in the sun we had been expecting.

The point of the story? It doesn't matter if you have a nice new anchor, if it won't attach securely to the bottom and hold you safe when the storms come; and faith is the same. Faith that is attached to the person of God is powerful and enduring. It will not fail you when the storms of life come. Why? Because of the very nature of who God is. Let's remember just who our God is:

'He spreads out the northern skies over empty space; he suspends the earth over nothing. He wraps up the waters in his clouds, yet the clouds do not burst under their weight. He covers the face of the

full moon, spreading his clouds over it. He marks out the horizon on the face of the waters for a boundary between light and darkness. The pillars of the heavens quake, aghast at his rebuke.' Job 26:7-11

'The Lord, the Lord, the compassionate and gracious God, slow to anger, abounding in love and faithfulness.' Exodus 34:6

'God is not human, that he should lie, not a human being, that he should change his mind. Does he speak and then not act? Does he promise and not fulfill?' Numbers 23:19

This is the One we fix our faith to. It's the awesome, powerful, omniscient, omnipotent omnipresent person of God, who is unchanging yesterday, today and forever He is worthy of our trust and our faith. It is He who gives our faith substance.

So in this book when we refer to faith, this is the faith we mean. Through this book we seek to share with you our experiences and learning of how we attach our faith to God, and how we develop the kind of faith relationship with God that will be an anchor that you can trust through the storms of life.

CHAPTER 5
Faith Lives Beyond Circumstances

Ever had a time in your life when everything just seemed to turn bad? Or when you received the worst news ever; or when the bottom dropped out of your world?

After eight years of preparation, we finally arrived at our first international posting in 1994. We had been in Outer Mongolia less than three months and were excited to see how God was going to move.

We were offered the chance to join our colleagues to check out an area being considered for the beginning of a new work. It was 400km east from Ulaan Baatar in a small town called Onderkhan, in the region where Chinggis Khaan was born. We jumped at it. The plan was to travel out and back by plane.

We hadn't even left the airport before the first crisis hit. Roaring down the runway about to lift off, the tyres on the left side of the plane blew and we slid around in a circle, coming to a sliding, screeching halt. We thought that was the end of the trip for the day; but no. They jacked up the plane with us still on it, replaced the wheels and tyres and away we went.

Left: STREET IN ONDERKHAN, MONGOLIA 1996

Falling from the sky

The time in Onderkhan went well. We were ready to jump on the plane and fly back to Ulaanbaatar. It was a small 17-seater Chinese/Canadian-built twin prop. As we stood on the rough dirt airstrip, I remember thinking there are far too many people here to fit on this plane. I just assumed they must be relatives come to say goodbye to family members.

As we boarded the plane, we were shocked to see everyone pile on board. Adults had one or two kids sitting on their knees; some adults shared a seat; and some just stood in the aisle. They even had three kids stuffed into the tiny cockpit with the pilot and co-pilot. As if this wasn't bad enough, they began passing huge metal milk cans filled with airak (fermented mares' milk) up the aisle.

Lisa leaned across to me and said, "I've counted, and there's at least 42 people on this flight. That cannot be good". I told her there was no way they would fly with this number of people; it would be far too dangerous. We spoke with our Mongolian co-worker about the number of people on the flight and at that moment he noticed the head of the airport coming toward the plane. To our relief, he assured us he would sort it out.

However, as he climbed on board and began to clamber over the containers, we realised he was so drunk that he could barely stand. Before we knew it, they had closed the door. The head of the airport threw up over some people as we taxied down the runway; people were pushing him around, as no one wanted him to fall on them. Then he passed out, and someone took his hat from his head and placed it over his face in a vain attempt to reduce the smell of the alcohol and vomit.

By this time, we had reached the end of the airstrip and begun to drive across the steppe trying to lift off; but with all the weight, the plane couldn't take off. All of a sudden, we hit a bump and literally bounced into the air. We were about 200 metres in the air when the plane went into a full stall. People were yelling and crying as the heavy milk cans all slid to the rear of the aircraft. In the cockpit the emergency alarms were going crazy and the pilots were yelling. One of them used his fist and started punching the console, hitting the buzzers to stop the noise, blood was pouring down his hand adding to the general panic in the plane. Fully stalled with the nose pointed straight up, the plane began to shake with such force we knew it was about to drop out of the sky.

Our American colleague was a pilot. His face suddenly became pale, and he calmly told us that the plane was going down. There is no way to recover from a stall at this altitude. Our Mongolian co-worker who was sitting behind us leaned forward and said, "You know this Jesus thing? Well, you guys have believed it for a long time, but what about me? I am only a new believer; is salvation going to work for me if we crash?"

Time almost stood still. It was that feeling you get when you watch something in slow motion.

I watched as Lisa assured our co-worker that Jesus knew what was in his heart, and that if this plane went down, God had us all in His hands. She prayed and talked calmly into the Walkman she always carried;...

I had been talking into my Walkman ever since I boarded the plane. I began to pray, and I said, "Please Lord; anything will do right now. I don't care what it is, but please just speak." What came to mind immediately was 'I have set my angels concerning you' Psalm 91; 11. I knew right at that moment that whether we lived or died, God clearly had us in the palm of His hands. I quickly began to tell my Mum and Dad on the Walkman how much I loved them, and that it would be ok if we died because God knew what He was doing; and that if we did crash, somehow I believed that God would get this tape to them. I spoke their address onto the Walkman, not expecting to walk away from the accident that was imminent.

Me? Well; this was far more than I was prepared to trust God for. My faith was not ready for this.

How much are we really prepared to trust God for? Trust Him to find you a carpark? Trust Him to heal your cold? Trust Him to restore your business or your marriage? Trust Him to bring you through a major illness? Trust Him if your child faced a life-threatening illness?

Trusting God is challenging because it raises the question: Is our faith based on our circumstance or do we have a faith that goes beyond circumstance? And is it possible to have such a faith without denying the reality of our situation?

Returning to the crashing plane-believe me, my eyes were firmly fixed on my circumstances and the reality of what was about to happen. I began to explain to God in the strongest language my situation and how unreasonable it all was. We had taken eight years of preparation getting ready to go to Mongolia; we'd studied for two years at Bible College, part of the time living in a 17ft caravan; we'd travelled all over New Zealand raising support, and had 30 churches signed up to support us. Arriving in Mongolia, we'd done three months of language study, and now…?

"It's unacceptable!" I raged to God, getting angrier and angrier at what I saw as the injustice of it all. (Just a word of advice… if you are moments away from your death and having to face judgement raging and telling the judge of your soul that He is acting in an unacceptable way, that is probably not a good idea! Just saying.'

42 PEOPLE PACKED INTO THIS LITTLE 17-SEATER PLANE

Fake Faith versus Faith…

To say I was having a crisis of faith, is an understatement. Why? Because my eyes were fixed firmly on the circumstances and my faith was based on God arranging what I considered to be acceptable circumstances. Faith that is based upon circumstance is really no faith at all. Can you take that in again… faith that is based upon circumstance is really no faith at all?

Even atheists have this kind of faith. Ever had a conversation with an atheist that goes like this: "If God would prove His existence to me, I would have faith in Him".

What they are really saying is if God would come into my circumstances and do some things that I think God should do, arranging my circumstances in the way I think they should be arranged, then I would say there is a God.

What's wrong with this thinking? If the next day my circumstances change and God does something that I don't think he should do, then is God no longer God?

Do I somehow control God? If I do, then is He really God the almighty all-powerful Creator of heaven and earth and of you and me?

For many people this is where their thinking about faith has become confused and where many have bought into the ATM Faith Machine discussed in the previous chapter.

Is our faith based entirely on hoping God will do what we want Him to do when we want it? Or worse, naming what we want God to do, when we want Him to do it, and believing if we only have enough faith God will have to do it, and we can claim it's already done?

Again what's wrong with this thinking? First, it denies reality. I claim my broken leg is now actually healed, even though it is still clearly broken. Seriously? That's not faith. That's just weird. No wonder non-believers sometimes shake their heads and wonder about us believers. We can be so weird at times.

Second, and more importantly, it leads us to a dead end, because who is able to control the thoughts and actions of God? None of us even knows the thoughts of God.

Isaiah 55:8-9 says: **'For my thoughts are not your thoughts, neither are your ways my ways," declares the Lord. As the heavens are** higher than the earth, so are my ways higher than your ways and my thoughts than your thoughts.'

So if you've been going along in your spiritual walk, believing you can somehow control God by faith and therefore control your circumstances, I'm sorry, but you're in for a huge disappointment. This kind of named or titled 'faith' leads us into crisis as soon as the circumstances don't fit what we think God should be doing.

Again, returning to the crashing plane. Why was I railing against God? Why was I in a crisis of faith? Because according to my understanding, this was not what was supposed to happen. We were supposed to have a long fruitful ministry in Mongolia where we would lead people to salvation in Christ, plant churches, train local pastors etc. Dying in a plane crash only three months after arriving, was not the way it was supposed to happen. And no amount of naming it and claiming it was going to keep that plane in the air.

Taken by Maoist Guerrillas

Let's fast forward eight years to 2002 in the remote North West highlands of Nepal, deep in Maoist guerrilla-controlled territory. This is the incident mentioned at the start of the first chapter of this book.

As mentioned earlier, we had moved to Nepal and I was leading the relief operations and security for a major international Christian aid and development agency. The conflict between the Government forces and the Maoists guerrillas was rapidly escalating toward civil war. Most international agencies had significantly reduced their operations outside of Kathmandu and other major Government controlled centres.

ROYAL NEPALI ARMY FIREBASE

I kept hearing about starvation and the lack of even basic medical care for children in the remote areas. We felt we couldn't sit comfortably in Kathmandu while we had the resources to save children from dying needlessly. The problem was access: how to get both sides in the conflict to agree to let us operate in these remote areas without interference. In later years I would become well known to the Maoist leadership and, as I have already said, I developed a variety of ways to make contact with them; but in the beginning it was very difficult.

My Nepali colleague and I decided to physically go into their territory to contact them. We understood the risk but had to weigh the lives of potentially thousands of children against the risk. Neither of us felt we could just sit by, we had to try. Full credit to my Nepali colleague, who is one of the bravest men I have met. He was always willing to put his life on the line if it meant we could save children's lives.

BUILDINGS DESTROYED IN THE FIGHTING IN JUMLA

We flew to the Jumla region in the north-west and set off into Maoist territory. Eventually we found the area commander, who was much less happy to see us than we were to see him. Believing us to be American spies working for the CIA, he felt the best option was to simply execute us.

As he was about to order his men to shoot us, I closed my eyes and all I could see was the face of Jesus. I remember praying, "This is it Lord; here I come! Catch me!"

The Maoist Commander paused and said, "Tell me why I shouldn't kill you". Time once again seemed to stop; but this time it was different to my experience with the crashing plane in Mongolia. I felt this incredible peace come over me. I felt a sadness that my life journey with Lisa was at an end and I would not get the chance to see my daughter grow up and walk her down the aisle one day; but there was no anger, and no crisis of faith.

Surprisingly, I was calm and ready to meet Jesus. But time had stopped, so I began to consider the commander's question. What could I possibly say to this man that would change his mind? I knew I only had one attempt to get this right. I began this strange conversation with the Holy Spirit, discussing various things I could say and discarding them one by one.

Jesus was serious when He said in Luke 12:11 **'When you are brought before synagogues, rulers and authorities, do not worry about how you will defend yourselves or what you will say, for the Holy Spirit will teach you at that time what you should say.'**

Eventually I felt the Holy Spirit give me the go-ahead. Knowing the Maoist's hatred of being called terrorists (they believed they were fighting for a better Nepal with an end to social and economic oppression) I replied, "Yes, you could kill us but that would be the act of a terrorist; and you're not terrorists, are you?"

This was the opening line of a dialogue with the Maoist leadership which, over the next three years, would open the way for us to bring food and medical assistance to tens of thousands of starving children and their families, caught in the crossfire of conflict.

The key to focusing on God, not circumstances

What was the difference between the crashing plane and the threatened Maoist execution? In the Mongolian plane, my eyes were on the circumstances; but in Nepal, my eyes were fixed on the person of Jesus. I had started to find a faith that could reach beyond my circumstances.

Working in developing countries and in war zones, you are never sure what's going to happen next, because circumstances change all the time. Things are not stable, and you have little control over what happens next. So I had begun to learn to put my faith in God and not in circumstances: to look to God, not to the situation.

The more we learn to live and act based upon who God is, not based on whether God is doing what we want Him to do in our lives, the more we can develop a faith that goes beyond circumstances. We learn to trust Him even in the bad times.

Sound good? So how do we do this?

The key is to submit everything to Him and hold nothing back. Every part of your life, your family, your work, everything!

It's kind of like a house. If you come by my house, I would easily welcome you into the lounge. We might sit in the kitchen and have a coffee. So far so good, but if you then wanted to go into our bedroom, I might start to get a bit anxious about whether we'd made the bed that morning. If you wanted to then go into the disaster zone called my teenage boy's room, I'd start to find excuses for why that was a really bad idea, and we shouldn't go there.

It's the same with God. There are areas of our lives we are comfortable to submit to Him, and then there are those areas we struggle with. We struggle because we hang on to areas of sin; we struggle because we feel it's too painful to go to some places; and we struggle to find the faith to fully hand over control of those areas which are dearest to us.

Isn't it strange how we will quite happily trust God for what will happen to us in the next life but struggle to trust Him for what's happening in this life? Why can we not just submit here and now, right now, today, this moment? Why is it always such a struggle?

I guess we love to cling to the self-deception that we have everything under control; and then we're surprised when life throws us a curveball we can't control. This is the simple truth: that if we will only let go and let Him, then our Heavenly Father will direct events according to His will, motivated and driven by His unending love for us.

Only on the other side of submission can we find His peace: a peace which passes all human understanding.[3]

> *This journey of ours challenged my faith in very different ways from Alex. Did I really trust my husband and friend into God's hands? I had to come to that place where I either fully believed we were in God's hands and I could surrender my family to God, or I knew we would have to leave and return to New Zealand.*
>
> *At the time this took place, I didn't actually know what had happened. However, I had always taken time to pray whenever he travelled away from home. Nepal was going through a very difficult time, and he was travelling through Nepal into areas that were not always safe.*
>
> *During all our time overseas, I had asked the Lord to lay Alex on my heart whenever something was not right. I clearly remember praying for him and having a heavy burden on my heart during this time. I remember receiving the call from him once when he and his team-mate had been released. He called me, and his voice was different; but he did not share what had gone on. He spoke to me in Mongolian, and I knew this meant that something was not right. He needed me to call his boss and pass along some information. The phone conversation ended; I felt a heavy weight on my heart. What could I do? All I could do was pray! Lord, do I trust you with Alex? There was no other choice. I remember committing him to God and asking God to fill me with His peace; and then I remember the*

---

3. Philippians 4:7

conversation I had with my brother: he asked, "What if something happens to Alex? How will you feel about God then?" All I could think of was: God, You brought us out here and I know Alex's time is not up until you say it is. I said out loud… **"You will keep me in perfect peace, and my mind is steadfast because I trust in You"** *(Isaiah 26:3).*

Ah… so you must be wondering if he is ever going to finish what happened to the plane. Well, clearly it didn't plummet to earth and burst into flames as expected, otherwise we wouldn't be writing this book.

An angel on each wing and two on the tail

As we all prayed expecting this to be our last moments on earth, all of a sudden, there was a large bump. We were thrown forward, and to everyone's surprise the tail end of the plane lifted. God must have had an angel on each wing and two on the tail because we started to move forward at a forty-five-degree angle. The pilot couldn't level out the plane, but he managed to fly it like this for an hour to Ulaan Baatar, and crash land on the runway.

When we landed in Ulaan Baatar, the whole airport had come out to see us. As we got off the plane people began to clap and cheer, congratulating the pilot for making it with all these extra people on board. We found out later that the practice at that time was to sell the legal tickets and then the pilots would sell extra tickets (called "rabbits under the table") to whoever wanted to fly standing up: the pilot would keep the money.

In a bizarre twist, I had totally forgotten that I told this story on this cassette tape in the Walkman. When it was full, I sent it off to my parents. As you can imagine; when they heard the story it really shocked them and immediately my Dad phoned me (at 2 a.m.) to say, "Don't you ever stay on a plane like that again if it is overloaded with people!" That was me told off.

CHAPTER 6
Developing an Authentic Faith

If developing a genuine authentic faith attached to God is all about the journey, what do the steps of that journey look like?

I remembered that when we were living and working in Nepal, a friend of mine called me up one day and said, "Hey, there's a couple of us going to climb up to base Camp on Mount Everest. Want to come with us?" There was no time to train or prepare and I was a bit worried at the thought of tackling the Himalayas again.

On my first trip a couple of years earlier, I had nearly died of altitude sickness I had travelled up on the Chinese side into Tibet by car, and ascending rapidly, I had been struck down by the most blinding headache (literally I couldn't see and couldn't stop vomiting). My companions raced me down the mountain to get me to a lower altitude, and on the way miraculously found a local Tibetan healer/doctor, who immediately gave me an evil-smelling concoction to drink. This knocked me out.

When I awoke, amazingly the headache was completely gone, without even a residue of pain. God is good, even at high altitude it seems, but I was still a bit nervous of what might happen this time.

Everest Base Camp

Before I knew it, I was on a plane landing at Lukla, which is in itself a crazy experience. The airstrip looks like it's carved into the mountainside, with steep ridges on both sides. You land going up the mountain, and you take off going down the mountain. When you take, off you don't really get enough airspeed to get fully airborne before you run out of airstrip (and mountain!) so you plunge downward until you get the lift needed to fly.

MOUNT EVEREST BASE CAMP 2003

I was a bit worried about whether I could make it all the way, but I soon got into the rhythm of trekking and was drawn into the magic of the journey. The amazing thing about trekking Everest, is the huge variety of terrain you walk through; from evergreen forests to tussock covered tundra, and finally steep valleys of rock and ice. The last part before base camp looks totally alien, like the surface of the moon.

The trail is very different as you go through each region. There are some parts where you stroll up nice gentle slopes, and other parts where you're climbing up steep rocky slopes, using your hands to pull yourself up. It wasn't until I had finished the trek that I realised the largest step I had taken was the decision to do it.

I guess every journey is like that, made up of different kinds of steps; and our spiritual journey in faith is the same. At times it is made up of easy steps when God leads us gently in small steps that we can manage, and then at other times it's made of giant leaps, when we feel we're leaping off the edge of a cliff. Both of these seem to be important for the journey of spiritual discovery God desires to take us on.

Of course, it's not really surprising that the most memorable steps, where we grow the most, tend to be those giant leaps, where we stand at the emotional cliff edge, teetering on the brink of our ability to trust God, but knowing He is calling us to let go.

Left: MOUNT EVEREST 2003

Stepping out in faith - A blind man healed

This is the way it has been in my life. I remember my second mission trip as a relatively inexperienced believer. We travelled to the south of the Philippines to Ozamis City on the island of Mindanao, where we were to spend some time serving a church there. I was excited but also a bit apprehensive. I remember thinking it'll be okay if I just stick to the practical stuff, maybe help them out in some practical ways working with the men in the church. Yeah, that'll be okay.

MINISTERING IN THE PHILIPPINES 1993

We had been doing practical jobs and helping with the youth and visiting families. So far it was going great. Then one day the pastor told us they were going to hold a crusade in one of the villages. We went along and helped them erect the stage and set up the sound gear and I thought this was going to be great to watch. The pastor had told us they expected between 1500 and 2000 people to attend and I was excited to see what God was going to do through the pastor and her team.

To my horror, she came to me minutes before the crusade was due to begin and said, "Brother, the Lord has told me that you need to give a testimony at this crusade today. When it's time I'll wave you on the stage, and you come and speak to the people". And with that she went on stage, before I could begin to protest that speaking to 1500-2000 people is not what I did, it was not me: I didn't even have anything prepared!

She introduced me and waved me on stage. I stumbled my way to the centre of the stage and mumbled out some sort of message or testimony. I don't really recall what I said but I don't think it was great. I was just thinking "I sure am glad that's over," when she said to the crowd "Now my brother here from New Zealand is going to pray for anyone who needs healing". I thought to myself "You have got to be joking! If speaking to a crowd like this was not me, then certainly stepping out in faith and praying for healing in front of a huge crowd like this was definitely not me.

LISA WITH A PHILIPPINES CONGREGATION

I remember putting my head down and beginning to pray and saying to God, "Okay God; this is really awkward. I have no idea what I'm doing here; so please just send someone forward who is easy. You know, like someone with a sore back or a headache or something. Something that I can manage "With that I looked up and to my horror I saw a man with a cane, completely blind in both eyes, tapping his way to the front. My response to God was "You have got to be joking; this is now no longer funny!" But what was I to do with all these people looking on expectantly?

I remember putting my hand on the man's shoulder and I wish I could say I spoke out a powerful faith-filled prayer of belief for his complete healing, but in reality, with my eyes closed what I said was… "God: okay… if You don't do something here You and I are going to look really stupid in front of all these people; so please just do something… anything!"

With that I heard the crowd begin to clap and cheer. I opened my eyes to see the man had thrown away his cane and was starting to yell something in the local language. It was then that it began to dawn on me that he had been completely healed and could see.

This set the tone for the rest of the trip. Again and again, we saw God move sovereignly, supernaturally, as we stepped out in faith.

At the end of our time in the Philippines, the pastor and her team wanted to bless us for all the work we had done and decided we were all going to go on a picnic, a fun day out on one of the islands off the coast of Mindanao.

The pastor had arranged a boat to take us to the island. It was a beautiful warm, sunny day, and the sea was calm. The sea and sky were a stunning blue and we felt we were in a warm relaxing blue bubble. We began to unwind after the full-on pace of the last week and let the sea and sun soak into our spirits.

A picnic gone wrong

Soon we arrived at the island, and we all took a lazy stroll to the local market to buy some fresh fruit to go with our picnic. We wandered through the bustling market, picking up some choice additions for our lunch, our minds wandering aimlessly when, without warning, the barrel of an M16 rifle rose levelled at my stomach. What was that doing here? What was happening? With a surge of adrenalin, a new reality came crashing into my consciousness. Before I could move, one of the pastors with us moved to place himself between me and the gun and a heated argument began in Filipino.

I could only catch the gunman repeating "Americano" and the pastor shaking his head and saying "New Zealand! New Zealand!" What I did clearly understand was the frantic hand signal he was giving me behind his back was go, go, go!

With that I jumped behind a group of local sellers who were selling something, I had no idea what they were selling, I just knew it was big and blocked the line of sight to the gunman. Grabbing Lisa, I sprinted out of the market spotting at least one other gunman. The rest of the church members were also moving and spurring us on with shouts of "run". "Go to the boat!" "You must get away!"

We really didn't need much encouragement as we ran flat out down the road towards the harbour. Keeping to the side of the road where we could dive into cover if we had to, we came upon an old warehouse. As we drew level with it, suddenly there was a crash of metal and a scream and the doors burst out towards us. I hit the ground not knowing what exactly had happened. I opened my eyes to find I was nose to nose, eyeball to eyeball, with the largest pig I had ever seen. It was trussed up and strapped to a trolley, clearly as freaked as I was.

Rather than something exploding, what had happened was the guy pushing the trolley had crashed it through the metal door and the pig was screaming its indignation at having to suffer such rough treatment on its way to be slaughtered.

I mentally pulled my heart out of my mouth, put it back where it belonged, somewhat sheepishly got to my feet and beat a hasty retreat to the harbour praying the pig and I wouldn't end the day the same way.

As we boarded our boat and headed out of the harbour, we learnt from our church friends the gunmen were members of Abu Sayyaf, who were hoping to kidnap Europeans; preferably Americans. Thank you, Lord, for the courage of our Filipino hosts, and for delivering us from what could have been a picnic gone badly wrong.

Smugglers for Jesus

From there we headed to Hong Kong where we experienced a very different kind of divine intervention. The agency we would be working with for a couple of weeks, had various mission programmes under way. We would be on the team smuggling bibles into China.

At that time the house church movement was really taking off and was under severe persecution from the Chinese authorities. Bibles and Christian teaching materials were badly needed by the young, rapidly growing, spiritually hungry church, but were banned by the authorities and therefore scarce. Some Christian agencies worked underground to smuggle bibles and teaching materials into China.

I'm not sure what I imagined we would be doing, but I guess I had thought it would involve avoiding Chinese border guards, not going through their checkpoints.

We wrapped the bibles in plastic bags and packed them in large suitcases (it looked like a suitcase full of bags of cocaine!) and were told we would be taking the train to the border, where we would cross into China at Guangzhou.

The team gathered together to pray and then we were given details of the route we would take. We were instructed to travel independently and not to acknowledge each other, so if we were under surveillance and one was taken, the others would not be compromised.

Honestly, the more questions I asked, the more the plan didn't make sense to me. In fact, it looked one-way trip to a China prison. I asked...

Would I go through the normal border crossing? Yes.

Were there scanners at the border? Yes.

Can the guards see the packages in the scanner? Yes.

It's forbidden to bring bibles into China? Yes.

Would we be arrested for smuggling? Yes.

Hmmm... I wish I could say, "It sounds like a plan!"

Just pray, have faith and trust the Lord to make the way... I was assured.

We set off, boarded the train and soon arrived at the border crossing. Waiting nervously in line, we avoided making eye contact with each other and prayed like crazy.

My turn. "Passport!" demanded the guard and slowly stamped my visa. Like a man in a waking dream, I put my suitcase up to go through the scanner. Lord this is crazy but here we go!

As my case disappeared into the scanner, my eyes were fixated on the face of the guard intently staring at the scanner's screen. I was waiting for his eyes to widen and his mouth to form the shout that would bring his companions crashing down on me. Nothing ……. No change. Just a blank stare.

I couldn't help it: as I walked through, I leaned forward to see if the screen was working. Yup. There it was. The image of my suitcase with all those bibles in packets looking more like packets of drugs than ever. How was this possible?

Pray, have faith, and trust the Lord to make the way… they said.

I grabbed my suitcase, hurried through and hailed a taxi. As instructed, I met up with Lisa and we changed taxis twice more before heading to the hotel to drop off our suitcases. At the hotel we met with the other members of our team. Turning on the television with the volume on max in case of surveillance, we made plans for the return trip.

We would make these trips several times over the next two weeks each time with the same result. It was real James Bond spy stuff; but James Bond has nothing on the awesome, supernatural power of God that we see as we step out in faith.

In Matthew 17:20 Jesus said… **"Because you have so little faith. Truly I tell you, if you have faith as small as a mustard seed, you can say to this mountain, 'Move from here to there,' and it will move. Nothing will be impossible for you."**

All it takes is for us to take the leap of faith. Too often we want to sit nice and comfortable, and say to God "Show us your faithfulness"; but faith doesn't work that way. Actually, this is the opposite of faith.

Hebrews 11:6 tells us that '**without faith it is impossible to please God, because anyone who comes to him must believe that he exists and that he rewards those who earnestly seek him.**'

So God says to us "This is the way it is, show me your faith and I will show you my faithfulness."

In Matthew 12:13, Jesus said to a man with a shrivelled hand, "**Stretch out your hand.**" He stretched it out, and it was completely restored, just as sound as the other.

In John 5: 8-9, Jesus said to the invalid by the pool at the Sheep Gate "**Get up! Pick up your mat and walk.**" and at once the man was cured; he picked up his mat and walked.

In each case Jesus instructs the person to take the step of faith and then we see the faithfulness of God.

Bloodshed and saving lives in a war-zone

During my time living in Jerusalem in 2014, I worked as the country director for a large international aid and development organisation. There were a few times when the conflict between Israel and Gaza flared up.

After a short exchange of rockets and bombs, things usually died down. While this always added to the suffering of the 1.5 million people held like prisoners in this tiny strip of land, blockaded on three sides by the Israeli military and the fourth by the Egyptian military, it usually meant suspending our work with children in Gaza for a few days and then going back to 'business as usual'.

In July 2014 it became clear the escalating conflict was not business as usual. We began to realise this time that what was developing was a full-on shooting war. As one Israeli newspaper in Jerusalem wrote 'Are we in a war in Gaza?' While the impact of the conflict on Israeli civilians from rocket attacks was minimal, we received increasing reports of Gazan families who had lost their homes and possessions to the Israeli bombing and shelling and were sheltering in sheds and garages without food or water.

The need was clear and so was the humanitarian imperative. Unlike most high intensity conflicts where the civilian population flees the fighting and aid agencies can provide assistance some distance away, in this case, the people of Gaza were not free to flee the fighting. Any assistance would have to be provided on the front line amid the bombing and shelling. The risk of humanitarian staff being killed or injured was high.

This led to one of the most difficult decisions of my life: whether to begin humanitarian relief operations in Gaza or not. I agonised over the decision, knowing the danger I would be putting my Gazan staff in. In the end I felt we couldn't ignore the growing numbers of desperate families, but I decided to ask only for volunteers. It wouldn't be right to compel someone to leave the relative shelter of their homes and move around the streets delivering food and water. To my surprise, the entire staff of our Gaza office came forward to volunteer. It was an amazing show of love and concern for the suffering of their community. I felt so proud of them and so humbled to have the opportunity to lead such people.

When a lull in the fighting came and I heard an armoured UN convoy was going to go into Gaza, I quickly put my name down to be included.

It wasn't an easy decision. I knew the risk that I might not return was high. Deciding to leave your family and go into danger for the sake of others, is something you need to know God is calling you to do. It's not something you do lightly. I still remember the pain of writing letters to Lisa and each of the kids to say a final goodbye in case I didn't return.

What happened next was the kind of comedy of errors I've only ever encountered in conflict zones. First the UN called me back to say they were short of seats and could I bring my own armoured vehicle - like I had an armoured vehicle parked in my garage. Then they called to say the other NGO's had decided not to send any staff so there was plenty of room. I said I was okay to go. Then they called to say the armoured convoy was cancelled as it was too risky to send UN staff, but a group of journalists still wanted to go. I said I would still go.

I said goodbye to my family with a sick feeling inside, knowing I might not see them again. If I did make it back, I wasn't sure when that might be. My courageous security coordinator had offered to drive me to the border to meet up with the journalists and so we set off in our totally un-armoured vehicle. Before we could reach the border area, suddenly there was the wail of sirens and the crump, crump of rockets. As I lay in a ditch at the side of the road watching the rockets landing around us, it all became very real.

Back once again in the vehicle, we finally reached the border area and were welcomed with another barrage of rockets. This time the nearby Israeli Patriot surface-to-air missile battery fired in response, their missiles shrieking overhead to take down several rockets, their white contrails streaming from rockets and missiles, with dirty white explosions wherever they connected. It was all happening so close to us that I felt like I could reach out and touch the missiles in flight.

Inside the Erez border crossing, I found the group of 30 journalists. The Israelis confirmed that an agreement with Hamas for a temporary ceasefire was now in place. This would allow us to cross into Gaza; but we had to move quickly. I lined up with the journalists to be processed through the checkpoint but immediately ran into difficulties, when the Israeli border guards realised that, unlike everyone else, I didn't have an international press card and I wasn't a journalist. This began half an hour of heated argument with the guards. They insisted no international humanitarian staff were going *into* Gaza. Some had been evacuated *out* of Gaza but there was no clearance for me to go in. I repeatedly insisted that clearance had been given through the UN and they should contact their HQ. Finally realising I wasn't going to disappear, they agreed to contact their senior officer, who confirmed I was cleared to enter Gaza.

As I left the crossing building to walk to the border wall, I realised with a sinking feeling, that there wasn't a single journalist to be seen anywhere and clearly I had missed my ride. To make things worse, the nearby Israeli artillery opened up and began to shell nearby. However, the thing that caused the fear and adrenaline rush that comes when you know you're in immediate danger, was that as I approached the final armoured door in the wall, I realised that the pinging I could hear was shrapnel from incoming rockets landing on the other side. With that, the armoured door began to roll back, and it was decision time; cut and run back to the relative safety of life in Jerusalem, or run through the door into the hell of no-man's-land.

So many things raced through my mind. The first being of course "Alex: what the hell have you got yourself into this time?"

This was the moment I stood on the cliff of indecision and had to commit. Do I take the leap of faith or not? You see I knew deep in my spirit that I had been called to take up this role in Palestine for a reason. During the previous four years under my leadership, we had been able to rebuild the office leadership, stabilise and then significantly increase our funding and programme size, and improve the quality and efficiency of our work; but I knew deep down inside that a time would come that would be the defining moment for why God called me to Jerusalem. That moment had finally arrived.

These crossroad moments, when we know that everything we've done in the past has led us to this point in time, and everything we will do in the future is dependent on the decision we make, are both terrifying and transformative, all at the same time. It's the moment where we either pass the test and soar on to new heights of faith and confidence in God's plan and provision for our lives, or we fail and sink back into the mud of mediocrity and purposeless existence.

So many thoughts and feelings were exploding in my head, but as I began to focus my thoughts on my team members waiting for me on the other side of no-man's-land, I was overtaken by the conviction that, live or die, this was the time to be bold and step out in faith. I had been called for such a time as this: to lead these people at this time.

As the gate rumbled open, I ran through… Nothing, no journalists, no transport, but plenty of incoming fire... I ran and dived into a drainage ditch. With that, the gate rumbled closed, sealing me into a hell of the crack of small arms, whump of artillery, mortars and rockets.

What now? It was almost 1km from the Erez crossing to the Hamas checkpoint area where I could link up with my team. I knew there was no way I could make it on foot. A lone figure moving on foot would for sure be mistaken for the enemy by both sides.

I was stuck. Was I mistaken? Lord; did I get this wrong? Am I not meant to be here at this time? The doubts started to flood in. Desperately trying to figure a way out in the midst of the cacophony of sounds of battle, I heard something that didn't belong… the whining buzz of a two-stroke motorcycle being ridden at max revs.

To my complete shock, screaming up the crossing walkway came a motorcycle and sidecar with the rider yelling "YALLAH, YALLAH! Let's go. Let's go!" I recognised the rider as a local guy who often helped with baggage and goods coming into Gaza. I jumped into the sidecar with a huge THANK YOU GOD. We took off at speed bouncing and weaving. Holding on as tight as I could I wasn't sure if I was about to become a casualty of war or of his insane driving! He took me to the abandoned Palestinian Authority checkpoint which was halfway across no-man's-land. There I met up with the journalists who had only made it this far before the firing started up.

For the next three hours, I crouched beside a 1m high block wall as shells and rockets crashed around. I had a front row view of the fighting as several Israeli armoured vehicles and engineering vehicles moved forward, only to be attacked at close range by Hamas fighters with RPGs.

I was wondering if I had gone from the frying pan into the fire, and if I was going to be stuck here forever, answering questions from 30 news-hungry journalists. Things became more bizarre as the fighting died down and a luxury tour bus came bounding out to us. The driver yelled for us to get in. Inside, I crouched down on the floor and put my backpack against the side. Although I was wearing a flak vest, I was the only one without a helmet and with the massive glass windows, so good for seeing panoramic views but so bad for stopping shrapnel, I was feeling very vulnerable.

Suddenly a mortar shell exploded less than 20 metres from my window, well within its kill radius. Everyone piled off the bus. The side of the bus should have been peppered with shrapnel and the windows shattered but as I ran my hand down the side of the bus, to my amazement there was not a mark on it. Again, THANK YOU GOD!

Eventually we jumped back on the bus and I arrived safely to link up with my Gaza team. There would be many more THANK YOU

GOD moments in the weeks ahead, and several other close calls from danger-close encounters with Israeli bombs and missiles.

At one point a 24 hour ceasefire was called. My courageous friend and colleague (the leader of our work in Gaza) and I thought it would be a good time to check the situation of a couple of the communities we worked with in the north of Gaza, to see what was left of the green houses and crops in our agriculture projects.

A DESTROYED AGRICULTURAL PROJECT

The destruction was huge. Greenhouses were destroyed and the crop land blasted, cratered by shells and even deliberately bulldozed over. As we stared in disbelief and horror at what remained of our efforts to help the people of Gaza to be sustainable in food production, suddenly there was a BOOM and a shell exploded near us. With years of experience commanding armoured vehicles during my time as an officer in the New Zealand army, I immediately recognised the squeal of tank tracks and saw an Israeli Merkava main battle tank moving towards us. As its coaxial machine gun opened up with a thud, thud, thud, thud, at us throwing up chunks of dirt around us, we knew it was time to go.

DEVASTATED NEIGHBOURHOOD IN GAZA AFTER ISRAELI SHELLING

We sprinted back to our vehicle, thinking that even if the crew couldn't see our international NGO logos on our vests and flak jackets, they would see the signage on the vehicle and know we were part of a humanitarian mission. But no. As we jumped into the vehicle, the firing continued. We put the pedal to the metal, bouncing and crashing through ditches and over piles of dirt and debris to escape the fire.

It didn't take long for us to be joined by other fleeing civilians who had returned to check what remained of their homes and possessions, thinking they would be safe during the cease fire. We began to realise this was not an isolated incident, but the beginning of another push by the Israelis. We continued into a built-up area now packed with fleeing civilians.

We knew from our recent experiences that to be in a crowded location was extremely dangerous, as it invited attention from the Israeli Air Force. On top of that, we were now clearly right on the front line, so it was time to get out straight away. At that moment however, a man jumped out in front of our vehicle, putting both hands on the hood yelling for us to stop. He came around to my colleague's window and there was a rapid exchange in Arabic which finished with him jumping in the back of the SUV. I recognised him as a farmer from one of our community agriculture committees and I asked my colleague if he needed a ride. To my shock, my colleague replied "No, no he is inviting us for coffee. It's almost coffee time: is it okay if we have coffee with him?" What! Coffee! Now! What about the tank? What about the Israeli advance and the collapse of the cease fire? What about all the civilians around us running for their lives?

It was so, so Gazan to show no fear and say "we will not miss our coffee just because the Israelis and Hamas want to have a war in our neighbourhood"; so, so middle eastern to shrug and say "Inshallah": as God wills. I have since learned that it's also typical of civilians caught in the middle of war zones. The world around you is out of control and terrible things are happening which you don't have the power to control, so you hold onto that which you can control. Each day of living is an act of defiance.

"Don't worry. He has an underground garage where we can hide the vehicle". So off we went to have coffee. We discovered we weren't the only ones invited for coffee. Soon there was a group of about a dozen men, some farmers, a doctor, a teacher, a writer; all gathered for their daily coffee ritual. We sat in the underground garage sipping coffee with the whump of explosions going on outside, the ground shaking and the occasional trickle of falling masonry from his house above us, discussing the war, politics, God and the weather. It was a surreal moment; but slowly I began to see it through the eyes of faith. This group of Muslim men from different backgrounds and different professions, with very different levels of education, all had one thing in common… faith.

Faith in the faithfulness of God. Faith that even though the world had gone crazy around them, they could sit down for coffee and be at peace, content in knowing God is faithful. It was a great lesson in faith, and can I say… the coffee was also great!

Throughout that whole terrible month, God was continually saying "show me your faith and I'll show you my faithfulness". At one point we had a New Zealand television crew with a well-known news presenter from one of our main national channels come to do a documentary about the war and what we were doing. I was worried, knowing we couldn't guarantee the safety of the crew; but at the same time I was desperate to do anything we could to try to stop the slaughter. The presenter and crew arrived safely and we began to show them the terrible impact the war was having on civilians. We showed them what we were doing to try to help those that were homeless, without food or water; and to relieve the suffering of the children by teaching parents how to help their children manage the horrors. Things were going well when we heard about the funeral of a Hamas militant that was going to be held in their home, just next to a market area. I wasn't happy about the possibility of a large crowd forming and the risk of being near crowds, but finally agreed we could go, as long as it was understood we would depart if a crowd gathered.

We got there early, and the crew got much of the footage they were after; when, as I feared, a crowd began to form. Time to go. I hustled the crew out of the market area and into our vehicles. We had barely gone two blocks when there was the whump of an airstrike and a rising plume of black smoke. Two minutes later and that would have been us. THANK YOU, LORD!

I could tell you more stories, but I think you get the idea. Again and again, God showed His faithfulness, protecting me and my entire team. The war was a terrible, senseless tragedy and we felt devastated to lose nine of our sponsored children killed by the Israeli aerial bombing and shelling; but during this whole month, as we found shelter for families, distributed food and water and helped children cope, not one member of my team was killed or injured.

God is still saying to you and me today "Show me your faith and I will show you my faithfulness."

Letters with final goodbyes

When we left Nepal it never dawned on me that we would end up back in another country, where there was a conflict that would impact on the family.

When we found out we were moving to Jerusalem, I was delighted. The Holy land! Wow! I was so excited that we would be living where Jesus lived. After living in such spiritually challenging places, I thought we would be in a place that was spiritually uplifting, where all our spiritual needs would be met, and we would enjoy the peace of Jerusalem. Little did I know that nothing could be further from the truth. When we arrived in Jerusalem, we soon quickly discovered that the tension between Palestinians and Israelis was very intense.

While Alex was the one going into Gaza, it was a huge challenge for me as a wife and mother, to step out and trust that God would take care of Alex and bring him back safely every time he went in.

In 2014 we were on holiday in Spain. We had only been there 4 or 5 days when we got word that things were starting to go terribly wrong. Intense fighting had broken out in Gaza with rocket attacks and air attacks happening between Gaza and Israel.

We knew we needed to head back home. We had heard from friends that even the area of town we were living in had been trashed. I remember thinking: what does that mean?

We arrived back in Jerusalem When we got to our area of town, there was a checkpoint set up. Israeli soldiers warned us not to go into the area. We explained we lived there, so eventually with some persuasion, they let us through. As we drove along the road toward our place, we realized it looked like a war zone. I felt stunned; I was shocked at what I was seeing. Power lines were down, the train stop was totally trashed. We had to drive up on the footpath to get past the burning tyres and piles of metal to get to our home.

Shufat, where we lived, is usually a bustling area with kids out playing, music blaring and shopkeepers out selling things on the road. It was deathly silent. I didn't know what to think.

We were told by our security team that we could not go out walking, we were to stay at home. Alex had to show me how to use a gas mask and we all practised sheltering in our safe room, which was our little bathroom. That's when it hit me that this was actually real. We talked about our security procedures, we stored food and water in the safe room and prepared our quick-run bags with our important documentation and essentials for a rapid evacuation.

Everything was spinning around in my head. I asked God, "What is happening? Please, God, keep my kids safe." I felt sick. I couldn't think straight. Alex assured me everything would be fine. I prayed long and hard, and wrote to our many friends around the world, asking them to pray.

Alex was still heading into work most days, but the eeriness of Jerusalem felt dark, cold and very lonely. When rockets began to land in Jerusalem, we felt the shake of our building. I remember taking the kids into the safe room; I felt scared and afraid, particularly for our kids, but you know that is the moment when you have to have a brave face for the kids. You put on a smile and just reassured them we will be fine, telling them dad will be home soon, it's gonna be okay.

At the same time, I knew deep within my spirit that God was watching over us.

Shortly after this, Alex came home from work saying the war on Gaza had intensified. I had already seen the news and knew deep down that he would need to and want to go into Gaza; this was why we came to Jerusalem in the first place, to help those who were really suffering.

This was another time I felt like I had to step out and trust God once again. It was one of those times I really wasn't sure if he would make it back home. In fact, it was so uncertain that before he left, he wrote a letter to each of the kids and myself saying his goodbyes.

Everything within me wanted to say, "Stay, don't go". Yet I knew this is what we were there for; and even our 16-year-old daughter said, "I guess if Dad doesn't go, we may as well go home to New Zealand".

We knew there would be a serious risk if he went. Deep within my heart I feared he wouldn't return, but I kept my eyes on God, continuing to trust Him for Alex, knowing that his time would not be up until God was ready to take him home. For me that meant knowing that, no matter where in the world God had us, He would not take Alex until it was his time to go.

While the phone lines were not great, I managed to speak to him once or twice during his time there. On the first phone call, he literally had just gone through the border crossing and was huddled down by the big metal door. I could hear bombing and shelling; my heart was racing. It was not easy to hear and he had to yell as the noise in the background was so loud and intense. Eventually he hung up. I remember feeling overwhelmed and so unsure if he would be ok. I went to my room, got down on my knees and prayed, just asking God to keep him in His hands.

I didn't know whether he would return or not, but I had come to learn that God's arms were the safest place I could trust my family into.

That time was such an intense time of trying not to worry, but the news of more and more fighting and lack of personal contact with Alex, had my heart beating rapidly. The result was that it drove me further into God's presence.

I'll never forget when he walked back in from that trip. We held each other for the longest time as we both cried. Although we hadn't talked much during that time, I could feel some of the pain he suffered at what he had seen. By God's grace, He had kept Alex and brought him home to us.

This scripture was brought to mind during this season. It was a reminder to me that keeping my mind fixed on Christ is the only way to find peace in a difficult situation.

'You will keep in perfect peace those whose minds are steadfast, because they trust in you. Trust in the Lord forever, for the Lord himself, is the Rock eternal.' Isaiah 26:3-4

Chapter 7
Faith to Trust God's Decisions

After five intense years, our time in Jerusalem was coming to an end for Alex and me. At the time I was laid up at home in Jerusalem with a badly broken leg that had me bed-ridden for three months, but the excitement about moving on was building inside of me. I knew our journey had not finished, and it was just a matter of working out with God where to go next. The only thing I knew was I did not want to move back to New Zealand. In fact, in my heart I had hoped that we would go to Lebanon. As a family we were praying for the right door to open.

I'll never forget the day Alex came home from the office saying he had been offered a job. I was so excited; I just knew it would be somewhere challenging as all our postings had been. That was the journey God had us on all these years. As a joke, I said to Alex "As long as it is not New Zealand", as I knew we wouldn't be going there.

He just went very quiet, I said to him, "You're joking right? There's no way I am going back to New Zealand". I remember feeling sick. How could this be? This cannot be God's direction for us. God, you know I'm comfortable here in these kinds of places. You know I feel safe and secure living in the unexpected. God, this can't be the right decision. This is not what I'd planned, and I'm pretty sure this is not your plan for us. Surely, God, this is a mistake?

I didn't want to go back home. I had felt it wasn't my home anymore. I didn't even feel like a Kiwi. I didn't know what would be expected of me and I was scared at the thought of starting over in what should feel familiar but actually felt far from that.

I just didn't want to discuss it. It was not an option for me. Not only did I not want to go, but I was determined to find somewhere else we could move to.

Then the Lord brought to mind an email which my mum had sent several months earlier. Mum would often bless me with encouraging emails, lots of them! As there were so many amazing emails she sent me, I often didn't get around to reading them until months later. Every now and again, one of them would catch my eye and I would save it in a separate folder. Sometime in the future I would get around to reading it. Well, this was one of those times. I was going through the email folders and saw the unopened message. I opened it and read it; it had a prophecy and a scripture and this is what it said:

"Now is the time to come back to the place I took you from. I am calling you home. You have become too comfortable and complacent where you are, and it's time. The fullness of My plan is ahead of you. The sweet taste of joy has filled your heart, but there is more for you as you leave the predictable and move forward. It is waiting for you: step into all that I have chosen to bring to pass in your life. Faith will not hesitate when My cloud has moved. I will direct you with My cloud and with My presence. Never be afraid to step out, and you will find more of me. I will be your peace and I have gone before you to prepare the way, for I delight in you and will never leave you; for you are Mine."

The verse of Scripture was...
'Not that I have already obtained all this, or have already arrived at my goal, but I press on to take hold of that for which Christ

Jesus took hold of me. Brothers and sisters, I do not consider myself yet to have taken hold of it. But one thing I do: Forgetting what is behind and straining toward what is ahead, I press on toward the goal to win the prize for which God has called me heavenward in Christ Jesus.' Philippians 3:12-14

I couldn't believe what I was reading. Could this really be God's plan for us? Could he really be calling us back to the place He called us out from? "God, how could this be? Surely you know this is not what I want. I'm not ready to face going back to New Zealand." I cried. What was I afraid of? Why didn't I want to accept this decision?

Yes, I was scared: scared of not knowing what the future would hold for me there. I had no qualifications; what would I do? I hadn't officially worked in the last 20 years. I had always volunteered and spent time getting to know people, just loving them for who they were and seeing how God might possibly use me in their lives; but that's not a job. Who's going to hire me for that? I didn't have any friends in Auckland. I simply didn't want to go, and neither did our daughter Monqtuya who was now 16 years old, and very angry at the thought of leaving and going to a country she had never felt a part of.

We were at an impasse. Lord; would I accept your decision knowing you hold our family's future in your hands, or would I push Alex into applying for a different position? I was torn. Everything within me wanted to say, "Tell them no, you won't go. We want to stay here in the Middle East". We had great friends, a great home and even though we never knew from one week to the next if there would be violence and conflict, we were comfortable. Why would we want to change that? I remember so clearly thinking "It's okay for Alex; he'll have a job. I'll be stuck at home. I'll never go out. I just don't want to go!" There were so many tears as I wrestled with God over this decision.

There were so many uncertainties.

What if we went and hated it?

What if we couldn't find a good school for the kids?

What if we made no friends?

What would I do?

Where would we live?

I felt insecure, lost and fearful of what the picture might look like.

Then I began to focus my mind on that email I had read. I could begin to see clearly that God had more for me, although at the time I couldn't picture anything. I surrendered my will, and accepted the decision that I felt the Lord had clearly placed before us. I began to get a peace about moving, and we started praying into the kids' schooling, housing, friendships etc.

One thing I had learnt from our 20 years overseas was that although Alex was often the one who was officially employed in a job, when God called us on to the next place, He wasn't just calling Alex; He was calling all of us. Every time we made a move in God, He provided the right friends, schools and place to live. He is faithful to meet our needs.

It's been five years now since we returned, and I cannot believe the journey we have been on since arriving back in New Zealand. God has planted us deeply in our community in south Auckland and opened up incredible opportunities to reach out and impact people.

WORKING WITH FAMILIES IN SOUTH AUCKLAND

I can't believe how God has been steadily building my confidence and preparing me for new areas of ministry. I now work for an organisation that is deeply embedded in the local community in which we live. We work to restore families, helping people see their potential and make life-changes that will change, not only their lives, but generations going forward.

God has opened up opportunities to connect with families in a way that may never have been possible, had we not been willing to move to the area in which we now live and fully trust God's decision. It was time for us to return. I'm so grateful that I was willing to surrender my desires for what God had planned for us. It's scary when you have to step out and trust God's decisions over your own, but I am reminded of Isaiah 55:8-9:

'For my thoughts are not your thoughts, neither are your ways my ways," declares the Lord. "As the heavens are higher than the earth, so are my ways higher than your ways and my thoughts than your thoughts.'

Deep down inside, I knew I could trust Him; but trust requires actively surrendering your will and choosing to let go of what seems sure and certain. It requires us to be open to something that may not look as if it has the right answers.

An even bigger test and struggle for me was the issue of having kids. When I was first married, I was so excited at the thought of starting my own family. I knew I was good with kids and I had always dreamed of having my own large family. From the time I was young, I had a series of baby-sitting jobs looking after other people's kids; and now it was going to be my turn.

Why God, why?

By the time we had been married a year, I had it all planned out: when we would fall pregnant, how many kids we would have; and how many years we would have between each child. But this plan of mine had one key ingredient missing. I had not asked the Lord what His plan for us was. It never dawned on me I wouldn't have kids when we planned.

I clearly remember thinking "Children are a gift from the Lord. Isn't that what the Bible[4] says? Why would God not want me to have kids?"

---

4. Psalm 127:3

We prayed with all confidence, trusting that God would give us the kids we desired at just the right time. So many times I let God know that surely the right time was in the next six months or so. Right?

After our first year of marriage, we were asked to consider doing part-time foster care for children who were being placed in the Government support system. It would give parents a break for up to a few weeks at a time. People told me "you should do this, as it will take your mind off being pregnant and then you'll easily fall pregnant". This somehow made sense to me at the time.

Weeks turned into months, which then turned into years. "God, where are you?" I asked. "Why are you punishing me? Do I not have enough faith?"

So many people asked "Don't you want to have kids? Why are you waiting so long to have kids? You just need to have faith. Have faith? I thought, do they even know the pain of watching your friends fall pregnant one after another, attending baby shower after baby shower and rejoicing for them; but deep down inside broken, feeling like you're not good enough, wondering what you did wrong?

During this time, we fostered more than fifteen children, ranging from one week old to twelve years old. So many children in pain, parents separated, mum or dad in prison. Alcohol and drugs tearing families apart. Taking in kids to give parents and children a break, was the least we felt we could do, and we wanted to do whatever we could do for these kids.

One of the children we fostered during this time, was a week-old baby. The baby stayed with us for three months. I couldn't help wondering: would this one become ours? No, God had prepared another family for him. We loved child after child who came into our home, and poured our lives into them. We did it faithfully for two years. When would it be my turn?

One night, at a meeting with some solo parents, I was sitting next to one solo mum with eight children. Six of them were in foster care because her life was such a mess. She kept falling pregnant and she told me you get good money out of the social welfare system when you keep having kids. I shook my head, "Why, God, would you allow a woman, who doesn't really even care about the kids she has, continue falling pregnant; but me, here I am, childless? Don't you see me waiting, longing, and hoping for a child of my own? How my heart aches! These children are born into homes of parents who can't cope. Some parents don't even want their children. God, do you not know I want one of my own? Don't you see my broken heart? I would love a baby; I would raise a baby right. Why, God? Why is this desire in my heart to have a family so strong? Yet I can't fall pregnant. I want to trust you, to hold onto faith, trusting that you have it in hand, but three years have passed now. How long do I wait?"

I was struggling to keep my faith. Then in that moment God spoke ever so quietly over the noise of the room and I heard, "Having children is such a small part of what I have for you." My heart leapt. "I know it is You, Lord; Your voice, without a doubt. Oh, wow; this means we are going to have our own kids: a big family," I thought.

I began to dream again; to hold onto that hope and trust in God once again. Maybe it's going to be this year? After four years of marriage, I can't wait.

During this time Alex and I had all the tests. There was no medical reason we couldn't have children. Then the doctor told me not all women have children, and asked if I had thought about in vitro fertilisation or adoption? What? "Seriously; why are you asking me this? Don't you know my God is bigger than this?" I thought.

Four, five, six years on, my faith started to waver once again, as more questions from church people, friends and family, came at me again. "We can't believe you have not fallen pregnant yet." Oh, how I wished they would understand the pain behind it all. Every movie I watched; they were having babies. Everyone I saw in the street had a pram, all adverts on television were about buying baby items. It hurt so much, I spent so many hours crying, pouring my heart out to God. Why, why, why? Just so many unanswered questions.

Finally, I surrendered it all again to God. I let go of the hope of having children of my own. It's okay, I told myself. I will just love my friends' children. So easy to say; so much harder to do.

By then we were living in Mongolia with all hope of having my own children gone. Well; surrendered, really; but with me trying to deal with a sense of ongoing pain and rejection. Then, all of a sudden, out of the blue, we got a phone call from a friend telling us she was pregnant and due to have twins soon. She was not in a place to care for them and was asking would we consider adopting them?

What an opportunity! I couldn't believe my ears. Was this for real? Alex and I talked, we cried, and we prayed. Oh, how desperately I wanted to say yes, to hold a baby that I could call my own. Was this the moment I had waited for? Was my faith being tested? After eleven years, was this God's promise from earlier years becoming a reality; that having children was to be such a small part of what He had for me?

After lots of time in prayer, I really felt the Lord say "You can do this. It's not right or wrong but it will not be my very best for you. If you take this option, you will be like Sarah and Abraham in the bible, looking for another way that is not my way; but you can choose. You are free to choose.

I was racked with doubt and indecision. What if I choose to let go of this opportunity, I may never get to hold a baby of my own. God, can I really dare to believe and have enough faith that you are still in this? Eleven years had passed, and I had tried holding onto faith; but my heart ached, feeling like I needed to accept that having kids would not be a part of our life.

I cried out to God, "Why are you testing me like this? It hurts, it's hard and every time I hold a friend's baby, I ache beyond belief." But how could I say yes? If this was not His best for us, why would I choose this option? I felt confused, afraid to let go and trust; but what else could I do? I wanted His very best for me. Finally, I chose to let go. I laid the idea of having a baby at His altar once again.

Back in New Zealand on furlough for a few months, I woke up one night after dreaming. Did I dream right? In my dream I felt God told me that the next time I came back to New Zealand, I would be pregnant. Could this be true? I thought maybe it was just my own desire to see this happen, so I returned to Mongolia and put the dream out of my mind. Unbelievably, eight weeks back at home in Mongolia, I found out I was six weeks pregnant.

That journey of waiting, trusting, daring to believe, and holding onto the hope and faith that one day I might hold my own child, was well worth the wait. On December 31st 1998, our beautiful girl Monqtuya was born. Yes, it was challenging. There were moments of fear, discouragement, sadness, and His timing was not what I had expected; and yet He was faithful.

You'd think by now people's questions would have stopped but no, as soon as Monqtuya was born, the questions began again. "Don't you want more than one?" My thoughts wandered, of course. I did want lots of kids. My thoughts started again. "Is it possible for me

God to trust you for another baby?"

As it turns out, I have found having faith to trust God's decisions means that things won't always go the way we think they should. Things do not always work out the way we want them to; but that doesn't mean they don't work out in the end, always better than our planning.

Following two miscarriages and at 41 years of age, my doctor told me I really shouldn't try to have any more children. With a family history of cancer and my struggles in this area, she did not recommend having any more kids. Heartbroken after nearly 21 years of marriage, I had only given birth to one child. I felt devastated, as I still longed for more children.

Monqtuya, who was nearly seven, reminded me of the word God had spoken back very early on. "Mum, you wrote in your bible that God had spoken to you about kids. He said that having children was such a small part of what He had for you". I said, "Yes, honey; and God has given us the most precious gift in you." But she said, "Mum that word you heard did not say a child, but it said children, so I know you will have another one." Oh, how precious that little girl's words were to me. Could this be true? Did I just need to continue to trust God and have faith?

I can't pretend that I really believed her; but on August 15th 2007, Zachary Alexander was born into our family: an awesome, talented boy with a great sense of humour. Who could have believed that this would have been our journey?

GOD'S PROMISE FULFILLED ……. IN HIS PERFECT TIMING

Now 13 years on, when I look back at the journey God has taken us on, I realise that had God given me what I had longed for - a big family with lots of kids - we could never have travelled the journey He had for us and we would never have stepped into the fullness of what God had planned for our lives. I'm so grateful God did not give me what I asked for in my timing. Faith is trusting that God really does have a plan and a purpose for us; but not in the way we often expect.

During this time there were a couple of Scriptures that really encouraged me. The first was Jeremiah 29:11-12:

'For I know the plans I have for you," declares the Lord, "plans to prosper you and not to harm you, plans to give you hope and a future. Then you will call on me and come and pray to me, and I will listen to you.'

The second Scripture is in 1 Samuel 1:1-20. Hannah had not been able to conceive for many years. She was fully committed to following God but deeply distressed because she had not fallen pregnant. She just kept pouring her soul out to the Lord through her tears and this made me feel it was okay to keep coming back to God with my tears and anguish.

Realising that God does have a purpose and a plan for our lives, helps each one of us to keep going and to keep trusting in Him.

HOT AIR BALLOONING IN TURKEY WITH OUR TWO RASCALS

CHAPTER 8
Faith and Suffering

Despite being part of a more enlightened world than the one our ancestors knew, there is still plenty of suffering in our world.

If you are white, middle class and had the good fortune to be born to a good family and live in a first world country, you personally may not be too familiar with suffering yet; but the reality is, no one is totally immune from it. Suffering is not a theoretical concept; it's something we all face sooner or later. Unfortunately, in my journey I have witnessed far too much of it.

I've wept with villagers who have lost family, homes and businesses in a tsunami. My heart's gone out to people desperately trying to locate family members after a cyclone. Even worse is the suffering caused by man's inhumanity to man. Women mutilated by crazy militia soldiers, their stomachs slashed open and their unborn children ripped from them and dashed against brick walls; and the children... I still get a tightness in my chest and a sick feeling in my stomach as I remember the terrible words of a guerrilla leader who told me "of course I use children for my personal guards. They are too stupid to be afraid and they always die for me without complaining". Or I remember the dead eyes of numb, unfeeling children in a Maoist 'enforcer' squad, whose job was to collect taxes and enforce compliance, terrorising villagers and beating them or chopping them into pieces with the large knives and kukris they carried.

Where is God in the midst of all this suffering? My worst memory, the one that still explodes into my mind when triggered by something on television or something I read, was the horror of a children's room in a house in Gaza during the 2014 Gaza war.

The suffering of the innocent

It was only just after 10 a.m., but the sun was already hot in the sky. There was a temporary ceasefire in place, and it seemed to be holding. My friend and co-worker and I took the opportunity to go to one of the neighbourhoods that had been hit hard by Israeli shelling and air attack.

We kept one eye on the Israeli drones incessantly buzzing above our heads, and the other eye open for troops and armoured vehicles that would open fire on us if we got too close. We carefully made our way through the piles of rubble and devastation. This rubble had once been a thriving neighbourhood, full of families each with their own hopes and dreams; families now as devastated as the buildings we passed.

We moved street by street looking for survivors badly in need of food, water and shelter and came upon an old woman with tears pouring down her wrinkled cheeks. She pleaded with us to help her dig the rest of her family out from the pile of rubble that until recently had been their family home. She was the only one to make it out when the shelling collapsed their home on top of the family sheltering inside. We could tell from the pungent smell of decaying bodies there was not much hope anyone was still alive, and we didn't have the necessary equipment to move the rubble; so we shared our water with her, told her where our distribution centre was, and urged her to go and find food, water and shelter there.

A WOMAN PLEADING FOR PEOPLE TO HELP SEARCH FOR HER FAMILY

We moved on to the next house, which was still largely intact. A man ran up to us, pleading with us to come to his home to see what had happened and to help his wife. As we went up the broken stairs, we could already smell blood and charred flesh. We entered his children's bedroom and were confronted with a scene from hell.

The charred dismembered body parts of four children were scattered around the room lying amongst their scattered toys. Hands shaking in rage, the father showed us where the Israeli Hellfire Missile had penetrated through the roof of their home. The mother, overcome by the horror, sobbed, screamed out in torment, and pleaded with us to tell her why? Why did this happen? What did the children do wrong? They were sleeping in their beds. Why did God allow this?

Even today as I remember the horrific sights, the tang of blood and the acrid smoke, I also remember feeling utterly helpless to make this right, of being incapable of giving any answer to the poor suffering mother that would in any way make sense of what had happened.

Difficult questions require answers

Is God responsible for suffering?

How did God allow this to happen?

Did God do this?

Does God cause suffering or is something else going on in the world today?

These questions are critical to our ability to place our faith in God. If unanswered, they can be an impossible barrier for non-believers to overcome. This can stop them from taking their first steps towards faith and can keep believers from fully embracing a love relationship with God. I don't know about you; but for me, if God is an angry guy sitting on His throne, throwing down wrath on innocent children, causing them to suffer and die horribly; then that's not someone I can put my faith in.

These questions raise all kinds of other uncomfortable questions about the character and nature of God, about God's sovereignty and about His judgement on mankind.

They challenge the relevance of our gospel. Is our gospel really good news for those who are suffering? Is our gospel big enough to embrace this kind of suffering? If it's not, then is our faith really relevant to a world filled with suffering?

Since my first encounters with extreme suffering, I've done a lot of praying and soul-searching. Many times I've been desperate for THE answer.

I still don't feel I have THE answer. If I've learnt anything, it's that there is no one simple answer. Rather than discovering a simple, straight forward answer, it seems we have to piece together several known truths, in faith

The most fundamental truth is that we don't fully know the mind of God. God in His fullness is a mystery. His ways are not our ways, His thoughts are not our thoughts. If they were, He would not be God. We would be God. However; we do know what God has revealed about His nature and character. This is summed up nicely in Exodus 34:6-7 when God says this to Moses about himself:

'The LORD, the LORD, the compassionate and gracious God, slow to anger, abounding in love and faithfulness, maintaining love to thousands and forgiving wickedness, rebellion and sin.'

So God is full of love for us, and in His love for us He offers us forgiveness. In fact, the entire Bible is the story of God extending his offer of love, forgiveness, blessing and protection; and mankind repeatedly rejecting it: something that continues today.

At the same time, the passage in Exodus 34 goes on to also say this about God's nature and character:

'Yet he does not leave the guilty unpunished; he punishes the children and their children for the sin of the parents to the third and fourth generation.'

There is also a righteous side to God that will not allow sin to go unpunished. We know there is a cost to sin, and the cost has the ability to affect not only what happens today but what will happen to future generations.

At the time I'm writing this, the world is going through the pain and suffering of the COVID 19 pandemic. This is a global crisis on a scale mankind hasn't experienced since WWII. It's not surprising that people are looking for answers to "why the loss of billions of dollars" or "the disruption of the lives of millions and the deaths of hundreds of thousands". Many people are asking if this is a curse God has sent upon mankind.

Does God want mankind to suffer?

The answer of course is absolutely no, He does not. The Bible is a record of God's efforts to SAVE mankind from suffering; to set up paths to deliver us from the suffering of our sin, and encourage and cajole us to use our freedom of choice to choose the way that will lead us away from the terrible cost of sin. We can hear God's heart in His words to the prophet Ezekiel in the book of Ezekiel 33:11

'Say to them, 'As surely as I live, declares the Sovereign LORD, I take no pleasure in the death of the wicked, but rather that they turn from their ways and live. Turn! Turn from your evil ways! Why will you die, people of Israel?'

God has gone to extreme measures to save us from suffering, even sending His own Son to suffer and die in our place. As John 3:16 states…

'For God so loved the world that he gave his one and only Son, that whoever believes in him shall not perish but have eternal life.'

If God's heart is to see an end to suffering, why is there still so much suffering in the world?

In my journey to understand faith and suffering, I've discovered what I believe are some of the pieces to answer this question.

The cost of sin

The first piece is: there's a cost to sin. The book of Romans 6:23 tells us the wages of sin is death. Not only is there a cost to sin, but death (and therefore suffering) is part of the cost. In Romans 8:21 and 22, the writer Paul takes this further, and reveals to us that all of creation is in bondage to the decay of sin; and it groans as if in the pains of childbirth.

Ever wondered why natural disasters have steadily become more frequent and are often of greater severity? Over the 20 years I worked in disaster relief, it was easy to see this reality on the ground. The trend of increasing cycles of drought, floods, cyclones, earthquakes and tsunamis is clear. Over a 21-year period, the international aid organisation I worked for went from needing the capacity to respond globally to one major disaster, to needing to be able to respond to four simultaneous large-scale disasters.

Our world is in bondage to the decaying effects of sin. As it groans and decays under the burden of mankind's sin, it produces suffering. In its fallen state there is much suffering. Drought, floods, earthquakes, tsunamis, volcanic eruptions all cause suffering.

Why doesn't God step into this process of decay and save mankind from this suffering? Well; His plan is to do just that.

In Revelations 21:1 John sees a vision of this happening and writes:

'Then I saw "a new heaven and a new earth, for the first heaven and the first earth had passed away.'

God eagerly waits for the day when He can reveal a new heaven and new earth, free from the decay of sin. The question for us is: will we have the faith to endure the present suffering and not lose heart while we wait for that day?

Why does God not stop suffering?

The second piece of the puzzle of faith and suffering, is to explore the question: Is God not capable of stopping our suffering now?

With the power God commands, of course He could sovereignly step in and force an end to our suffering today. He has the power to do that. Then the real question is: when God has the power to force an end to suffering, why doesn't he?

I've begun to understand that the answer to this question takes us to a deeper understanding of just how much God loves us.

As I've shared above, my worst experiences of horrific suffering, have been as a result of man's inhumanity to man. Mankind seems to have an endless capacity to cause suffering to others.

As mankind has rejected God, rejected His sovereignty and rejected His ways of living, we have set up economic systems designed to enrich some, at the expense of others. Some of these systems never question the pursuit of wealth and refuse to consider the morality of what they are doing. These include systems that are built upon the unrestrained exploitation of natural resources, exploitation of vulnerable populations and even exploitation of children.

We set up societies that glorify the material over the spiritual, that encourage all kinds of immortality and perversion, even to the killing of our unborn children. We are driven to indulge in levels of violence that defy reason; by religion, politics, tribalism, racism, nationalism, or any other 'ism' we can come up with. At every step, we sow the seeds of our own destruction.

And even though it pains God to see mankind suffering, He endures the pain because He refuses to destroy His creation by removing that which makes us uniquely us: the ability to reason and choose. He refuses to take away our ability to choose, because ultimately His desire is for us to choose Him.

In Revelation 3:20 God says: **"Here I am! I stand at the door and knock. If anyone hears my voice and opens the door, I will come in and eat with that person, and they with me."**

God won't break the door down. He waits to be invited into our lives. Another way the Bible describes this is by picturing God as a bridegroom waiting for His bride: Revelations 19:7… **"Let us rejoice and be glad and give him glory! For the wedding of the Lamb has come, and His bride has made herself ready. Fine linen**[5]**, bright and clean, was given her to wear."**

Then further on in the book of Revelation, we have the description of a beautiful day when all who have chosen God are finally fully reunited with Him, and all their suffering ends.

---

5. Fine linen stands for the righteous acts of God's holy people.

"I saw the Holy City, the new Jerusalem, coming down out of heaven from God, prepared as a bride beautifully dressed for her husband. And I heard a loud voice from the throne saying, "Look! God's dwelling place is now among the people, and he will dwell with them. They will be his people, and God himself will be with them and be their God. 'He will wipe every tear from their eyes. There will be no more death' or mourning or crying or pain, for the old order of things has passed away." Revelations 21:2

This is the centre of God's heart, with His deep, deep love for us. This is the end game God is committed to, and He will not allow anything to prevent this day from happening, even if He must witness our suffering along the way.

The third and strangest piece to the puzzle of faith and suffering, the one that can be hardest to get our mind around, is the reality that suffering, with all its pain, sense of loss, confusion and stress, can actually be good for us and is key to our growth and spiritual maturity.

With suffering there is hope

It was late in the year 2017. I was sitting in a refugee camp in Bangladesh, just across the border from Myanmar. I was working to raise international awareness of the horrors of the genocide taking place in Rohingya villages just a few kilometres away. As I watched the lines of shattered refugees making their way across the delta and sat with family after family, I began to realise the full scale of the horror that had been visited upon these people by the Myanmar military and civilians.

Hundreds of Rohingya men had been rounded up and executed in mass shootings by the Myanmar military. Dozens of women and young girls were raped and mutilated by soldiers, grabbed and held by their non-Rohingya neighbours, who were celebrating while they did it with music and festivities in a sick, twisted, hateful orgy of violence.

The shock and disbelief were clearly written on the faces around me. I sat on a hill alongside a child-sized grave in one of the refugee camps, sheltering more than 400,000 people. Surrounded by the scores of graves of those who had made it to the camp, only to succumb to their injuries or sickness, I felt a crushing weight of sadness, a deep aching in my spirit. It was an unbearable wave of suffering. If I was emotionally drowning and struggling to bear the pain of it just sitting on the fringe of this wave; what must it be like for those who had been caught in the full force of the suffering? Unbearable pain.

Boarding my flight home, I had time to go over my notes and reflect. As I went over the camp mortality rates, it struck me with all the emotional trauma and suffering, there was not one mention of suicide. I thought about my home country of New Zealand. 'God's Own': a place blessed with peace and prosperity; a place where children can dream, and everyone is free to make dreams come true. It's not that there is no suffering in New Zealand - there is. There is poverty, inequality and family violence; but as a country, we don't know what it is to experience the kind of suffering I had just witnessed.

And yet we have one of the highest suicide rates in the world. How is this possible? No one seems to have an answer for this deadly dilemma. In a society where most people have everything they need, why are large numbers of people in a state of despair and ready to end it all? And why in a Rohingya refugee camp, where people have just gone through the worst kind of suffering, is no one thinking of ending it all?

I'm still as perplexed as everyone else but I suspect it has something to do with the strange reality, that hard-wired into us as human beings, is the need to overcome adversity and face significant challenges. We don't seem to do well in an environment where life is easy. Utopia may be a nice concept, but it seems to be one that is insidiously destructive to us.

For us to be emotionally healthy, it seems we need to be locked in a struggle to survive, to overcome, and to prevail against the odds.

I guess this is what Paul meant when he wrote in Romans 5:3-5:

"**Not only so, but we also glory in our sufferings, because we know that suffering produces perseverance; perseverance, character; and character, hope. And hope does not put us to shame, because God's love has been poured out into our hearts through the Holy Spirit, who has been given to us.**"

With suffering there is hope; without suffering there is no hope. As strange as it is to try to understand, this is a deep truth which we must decide to accept and embrace in our lives, if we are to live as people of hope. God can use the mechanism of suffering to build our ability to persevere, build our ability to face adversity and build our strength to overcome challenges. God can mature our character, helping us to move from weak-willed, fearful spiritual babies, only focused on our needs, crying for mother's milk, into people of strong, rich character; courageous, mature believers focused on living out God's will for our lives. This process of transformation is where hope emerges and is sustained.

But it doesn't happen automatically. We must be willing to look for God's instruction in the midst of our suffering, and be willing to open ourselves up to it. We have to give God a free hand to teach and mature us, allowing perseverance to complete its work of maturing us, as the Book of James says:

'**Consider it pure joy, my brothers and sisters, whenever you face trials of many kinds, because you know that the testing of your faith produces perseverance. Let perseverance finish its work so that you may be mature and complete, not lacking anything.**' James 1:2-4

Riding with a message of hope

One morning I was on my way from my home in South Auckland to Tauranga, where I was to be the keynote speaker at a conference. I opened the throttle on my Triumph Commander motorcycle, letting loose the full power of its 1700cc twin engine, thoroughly enjoying the early morning sun and the sense of freedom that being on the bike always brings me.

The kilometres rapidly disappeared beneath my wheels and I was making good time, so I decided to stop halfway at a café in a small town called Matamata for a quick breakfast.

The event organisers had been a bit anxious about my riding down on the morning of the conference, and had made me solemnly promise not to be late; but I figured I had time for a quick bite.

Breakfast was everything you'd hope for in a small country town cafe café, and I was walking out to jump back on the bike, when an older man angrily yelled out across the room at me: "You know that cross on your back is a lie".

Now I'm a member of 'The Redeemed' motorcycle ministry: a ministry that was founded by ex-outlaw MC (motorcycle clubs) and gang members, who had encountered the transforming power of Jesus and gone through radical life changes. They still maintained strong ties among MCs and gangs, to be there for others wanting to make the same journey of transformation.

The way we dress and the way we ride, makes it hard to tell the difference between us and other MCs, but part of the ministry is declaring the lordship of Jesus Christ by wearing a large white cross and the words 'Jesus is Lord' on the backs of our jackets (we call it a banner, not patch; and it has no location rockers, to avoid any turf issues with other MCs).

NEW ZEALAND MOTORCYCLE MINISTRY

Wearing the banner often provokes a reaction (surprisingly mostly positive) in people, so wearing the banner in a confronting situation was nothing new to me; but it was unusual to be confronted by a well-dressed older man.

Mindful of the minutes ticking by, I briefly replied that the cross had made a real difference in my life and the lives of my brothers and so the promise of the cross was no lie. With that I jumped on my bike and headed out of town.

Ever had that sick feeling in the pit of your stomach when you know you've screwed up? Heading down the road, I could almost hear God sigh at the missed opportunity. Then this led to one of those really awkward God conversations.

"God, be reasonable! You know I'm the keynote speaker, I've got to get there on time. I know all that stuff you said about leaving the 99 sheep for the one lost; but the conference is important… isn't it? Then I repeated myself as if God was not hearing me… Isn't it? …….. Oh, all right, all right God. I screwed up! So what am I going to do about it, you say? What am I going to do about it? I don't know. I'll never get back there and make the conference on time and …… he's probably already left the cafe. So ………. Grrrr! alright. I'm going."

And with that I pulled a quick U-turn and roared back to town making good use of all 1700cc.

I arrived outside the café just the second the guy was leaving. As I parked up on the main street and pulled off my helmet, he came over, looking confused and said, "I thought you left". Great; I found him. But what now? All I had been thinking about was getting back to town, trying to find the guy and about moaning to God how this was seriously messing with my morning. So now God had carefully arranged a second encounter with him, and I had no clue what I was supposed to say.

I felt God say, "Keep it simple. Just tell him how much I love him". So, a bit awkwardly, I told him "I really felt God told me to come back and tell you how much He loves you. He really wants you to know how important you are to Him and how deeply He loves you." Well …… the transformation was immediate; and not in a good way. His face contorted and turned bright red with pure rage… this was seriously on the scale of Bruce Banner transforming into the Hulk. This mild-mannered old man switched into an inferno of pent-up anger. He balled up his fists, yelling at me at the top of his lungs, threatening to punch me in the face if I said that again.

MOTORCYCLE MINISTRY

Well; two things occurred to me at this point. One, looking at the shocked reaction of the bystanders, this was probably not something that happened often early in the morning in this sleepy town; and two, man I wish I'd left my helmet on!

While this was definitely not what I expected, I knew God had me there for a reason; so I pressed in and told him he could punch me all he needed to, but that wouldn't change the reality of God's love for him. As he pulled back his fist to take a swing, suddenly the dam inside of him burst open… "God isn't love! God doesn't love anyone! God doesn't know how to love anyone! If He did, He wouldn't have taken my little girl from me. All that prayer, all that pleading, and still He let her die!"

There it was... Years before, he'd lost a grandchild to a painful illness. He blamed God, and his pain turned to rage and bitterness toward God. All this time he'd been nursing his anger towards God; but all that anger hadn't brought his granddaughter back. It just led to a second death. The death of his relationship with God, and the death of hope.

God in the midst of suffering

Imagine, if instead he had been able to see God in the midst of his pain and suffering, to reach out to Him and receive His peace and healing, rather than remain wounded, he could have learnt a new level of perseverance. He could have experienced maturing in his faith and character and found hope, even been able to help his family and others to heal from similar suffering experiences and find hope.

I want to be clear. I don't hold even an ounce of judgement on this man. God forbid I should ever have to face what he faced. Pain and suffering are real. The struggle to find God in the midst of it is real. We all have a limit to how much suffering we can stand. But this doesn't change the reality that in the midst of suffering we only have two choices... reject God and take the path that leads to anger, bitterness and hopelessness; or press into God to find Him in the midst of suffering, to look to Him to help us persevere, grow through the pain and find hope.

If you've lost a loved one and know what it is to be overwhelmed by what feels like an endless all-consuming wave of grief and despair, then you know what I'm talking about. To drown in a sea of pain and despair and reach the point where you feel you can't take another step, you can't even breathe. When everything around us seems like it's breaking apart.

There... is... God.

He is right beside you. His arm is around you. His spirit is pressing in around you. He is with you. He has always been with you. He will always be with you.

Just as God turned me around to ride back to pursue a desperately hurting man in Matamata, He is pursuing you. You are His lost sheep; He feels your pain.

He has brought me on a thirty-year journey around the world to be at a place where I can write these words, so you would know He is here for you. He's not distant, unfeeling or uncaring. He loves you and He desires to lift you up from all of the pain and despair, if you will let Him.

If you will open up to Him, then just as your reality shifted on the day the pain and suffering began, it will shift again. As promised in the Book of Isaiah 61:3, He will bestow on you a crown of beauty instead of ashes, the oil of gladness instead of mourning, and a garment of praise instead of a spirit of despair. You will be called an oak of righteousness, a planting of the LORD for the display of his splendour. This may seem impossible with what you are feeling now and it takes time. There are no quick fixes to working through our pain and loss; but if you will just take the first step, you will see what God will do. This is His promise to you; and He always keeps His promises.

God's Love Abounds

I once had an astonishing conversation with a Nicobari man in an IDP (Internally Displaced Person) camp in the Andaman Islands. The terrible Asia Tsunami of 26 Dec 2004 had just struck, destroying communities and shattering the lives of hundreds of thousands of coastal villagers.

As part of the global rapid response team of a large international aide and development organisation, I had been immediately deployed to the Andaman Islands located just north of the epicentre of the earthquake.

A 15m high wave had smashed its way through the island's coastal towns and villages. The force of the wave had been unimaginable. I remember the first village I visited. We were walking to the village and I thought we must be getting close, because we had obviously arrived at the village rubbish dump. There were piles of debris, broken furniture, smashed cars, and washing machines etc., all around. When I asked how much further to the village, my local colleagues looked at me in surprise and told me we were standing in the middle of the village square. There was no structure above waist height left. In other parts of the island, I saw fishing boats tossed into trees and up on the roof of a school, the metal piping of the hand-rail from the concrete quay ripped out and rolled up in a giant ball: all were testimony to the terrible power of the wave.

I had been tasked with leading the organisation's relief efforts in the islands. This was a challenge, to say the least. How do you help villagers when there is no village anymore? Even getting to the islands was a challenge. Twelve hours after the disaster, I had been all set to get an emergency visa and jump on a plane, when the Indian Government announced that, as a regional superpower, that they did not require the assistance of the international community and my visa as an international relief worker was rejected. At that stage the true magnitude of the devastation was not clear, but it wouldn't take long for all the affected countries to realise that no one had the resources to respond to such large-scale destruction, without the support of the international community.

As a compromise, I was issued a tourist visa for the purpose of having a holiday in the devastated islands. I boarded the empty flight to the islands. This flight would return to the mainland full of evacuees. Not surprisingly I was the only tourist to arrive in the islands at that time. This began a bizarre drama, where for the next month, I would officially play the role of a tourist while arranging for relief goods to be brought to the islands and distributed; setting up IDP camps, building temporary shelters, etc. The Indian Government knew exactly what I was doing, but this way I was able to be sensitive to the Government's position on overseas assistance, everyone was honoured, and we got the job of helping thousands of desperate people done.

Left: VICTIMS OF TSUNAMI RELIEF, INDIA

I've almost always found respecting and working with local governing authorities to be a more effective approach than working against them. It's a lesson I learned early in my career, but one which unfortunately some of my colleagues in other relief agencies arrogantly disregard. Not long after we set up operations, another big-name, Nobel prize-winning international agency arrived without government approval. 24 hours later, they were sent packing, leaving hundreds of thousands of dollars of illegally imported medical aid lying on the airport tarmac.

I had encountered this agency previously in Nepal. I had been able to gain access to villages deep within the Maoist guerrilla areas of control and make arrangements with the Nepali government forces for our medical teams and food distribution to reach suffering children, who were innocent victims of the conflict. It had taken months of careful work, establishing relationships and building trust, getting everyone to understand we were neutral in the conflict. We were just there for the kids. When this agency arrived in the country, they also wanted to work in this same difficult-to-reach area. I sat down with their director and carefully explained how to go about gaining access and the importance of respecting the guerrillas, the military and the community leaders. Unfortunately, my advice was ignored. Within a few weeks of them trying to get set up, the Maoists were threatening to shoot them, the Army had arrested at least one staff member and the community had rioted and locked them out of their offices. The lesson for international agencies is that it doesn't matter how many Nobel prizes you win, if you don't learn that a little humility and respect goes a long way.

CALCULATING RATIONS IN THE ANDAMAN ISLANDS

Coming back to the Andaman Islands: I was working daily in the IDP camp supervising relief efforts and I saw that the Nicobari people, who come from the south of the island chain are Christian. Despite the horrors of what they had just been through, each evening they would gather together and have a time of worship, thanking and praising God.

One evening I got talking to one of the men in the camp. He told me how terrible the wave had been; how he had lost his wife, his two young daughters and his father. He had lost his home, his business and all his possessions. He was now alone with no surviving family members and he only had the clothes he was dressed in: one t-shirt and a lungi.

Then he began to sing and join in the worship. I couldn't believe it. The man had lost everything and here he was, praising God. How was it possible to suffer so much and still reach out to God? I had to know; and I will never forget his answer. "Alex; I have lost so much this week that I cannot afford to lose my God".

What a deep, deep truth. When we are in the midst of suffering loss, we CANNOT afford to also lose connection to our God, the source of our comfort and peace.

In writing this I have had two occasions recently to put this into practice in my own life.

In May of 2020 my father-in-law Mac passed away. My own father left when I was 14 years old, declaring I was no longer a son of his. By the time I met Lisa as an angry, hurt young man running from one emotional train wreck to the next, I had managed to successfully screw up every relationship with a woman that had even the remotest possibility of going somewhere.

Nevertheless, I was somehow optimistic, and one day expected I would find a wife. What I didn't expect to find was a father at the same time. I'll never forget the day I approached Mac, with a sick nervous weight in the pit of my stomach, to ask his permission to ask his daughter to marry me.

Despite assurances from Lisa, I was sure he would see through me; that he would see me for the fraud I knew myself to be. There would be no fooling him. He would see me for the violent lying, cheating, partying, woman-chaser I was. He would see I had few morals or ethics and fewer prospects. What could I possibly offer his daughter or his family? Of course, he would reject me; as so many others had, and as my own father had. Who would blame him?

As we sat down around a garden table and began to talk, he laid out everything he expected from a future son in law. It slowly began to dawn on me the conversation was taking a very different turn from what I had expected. This was not rejection. This was a conversation about the future: a future that I was invited to be part of. I quickly shelved the reply I had previously rehearsed about where and how he could stick his family, and haltingly began to talk about what I expected… no ……… what I longed for in a father.

His final words still echo in my mind. "Son: from now on, no matter what happens with your relationship with Lisa, I'll treat you as one of my own sons. No different from my other sons."

This sentiment was repeated at our wedding. He spoke at our reception, telling everyone that he considered his family to be like the All Blacks rugby team: in his words "hard to get into, but a hell of a lot harder to leave!"

So my relationship with my father-in-law was the closest thing I had to a real father. He was the one who fully accepted me as a young man. Not only did he accept me, but he taught me what it is to be a man of integrity: that a man's word IS his bond; that a man's worth is not measured by money or possessions, but by his reputation. He taught me the value of family and that it's a man's job to work hard to love and provide for his family, and to protect them at all costs. He saw potential in me, and believed I had what it takes to be a leader and make a difference in the world.

I miss Dad, and it hurts sooo much. His leaving has left such a hole in my world. This life will never be the same without him in it. He was always someone who was larger than life, and the world has diminished with his passing.

And yet I can see God's hand so clearly at work in His passing. His heart was failing; he was spared a long painful death in hospital. God took him quickly when he was sitting in his favourite chair. In the days leading up to his death, he had asked my mother-in-law to anoint him and pray for him. There is no doubt in my mind he was prepared to pass on to the loving arms of Jesus.

What's more, so much of him lives on in the lives of myself, his sons, daughter, daughter in laws, and his grandchildren. While in his day he was a huge figure in the New Zealand Dairy industry, leading New Zealand's largest dairy company, and was also a leading figure in New Zealand's economy at the time, this is not where his legacy lies. The strength of his legacy is in what he poured into the lives of his children and grandchildren and into all those fortunate enough to have him as part of their lives. Everything he put into our lives continues to bear fruit and will continue to do so, as we input into the lives around us.

Left: DAD - HIS LEGACY LIVES ON

Working through the grief, I've found myself a bit like a planet in orbit around the sun, as I emotionally orbit around my loving Heavenly Father: at times warmed by his love and comfort before drifting away, only to run back to the warmth of his embrace.

The second life-changing event I had to face was in 2019 when I found myself sitting in a doctor's office, being told it was likely I had lung cancer and needed a major operation that would remove at least twenty percent of my lung. The doctors couldn't do a biopsy because of where the lump was located, and they weren't sure how widespread the cancer might be.

This was not a good day in anyone's book. As the doctor continued to talk about the percentage chance of this and that, I stopped listening to him and started a conversation with God. There was no denying the reality and gravity of the situation but, as I started to focus on God, I knew I had two choices. I could focus on the terrible news or I could reach out to God in faith. As I reached out to God, his peace filled me and I remember saying, "Well, God, it'll be interesting to see what you're going to do with this one."

God was still God. He was still in His heaven. He was still the sovereign Lord of my life. While potentially everything had changed for me, nothing had changed for God. The only question was whether I would take the leap of faith and trust Him in this crisis. Could I find Him in the midst of this?

People started praying for me and believing for a divine healing that would save me from difficult and painful surgery and the potential of a painful, life-threatening illness. As I began to look for God in the midst of this crisis, I began to feel His peace and an assurance that, though I would have to walk through this, He was in control.

I went through the surgery and they removed the lump with a good portion of my right lung. I worked through a long, painful recovery process, which has left me less capable physically, than before. There were times of intense frustration as I struggled to come off the painkillers and come to terms with my new decreased level of physical ability.

But I was able to experience God in the midst of the suffering. God taught me a new level of perseverance; how to push back the horizon of what I can persevere against. As a young officer in the military, I had learnt to persevere for days and weeks in difficult conditions and later working in conflict zones I had learnt to persevere for months with extreme stress. Now God was teaching me to persevere against something which will likely affect me for years.

I noticed changes in my attitudes and thinking. Some changes were small and subtle: more determination not to miss opportunities to make a difference; a stronger focus on passing on what I have learnt (like writing this book for example). Some were more fundamental, like a total rethink about pastoral care and the importance of supporting those going through major health issues. Hospital visitation went from the bottom, to the top of my list of priorities!

It confirmed for me that we can find God in the midst of suffering, and God can use suffering to teach us and cause us to grow spiritually if we will allow Him to.

I had long been familiar with Romans 8:28

'And we know that in all things God works for the good of those who love him, who have been called according to his purpose.'

But, like many believers, for years I had wrongly understood this to mean that as a believer I won't go through hard times. Now I've realised it's not about getting a free ticket to bypass suffering. It's about going through suffering. It's about: how if we let God; then He will stretch us, grow us and mature us through the suffering. We are never alone in our suffering.

This is something all believers can take strength and comfort from and is described beautifully in the book of Philippians 1:6 **'Being confident of this, that he who began a good work in you will carry it on to completion until the day of Christ Jesus.'**

> *I have been through my own share of struggles, feeling pain and seeing suffering around me. It's been from a different perspective from Alex, though, and I am sharing some of things I have seen and experienced.*
>
> *In Mongolia, it's true the winters were very harsh; and as we shared earlier, temperatures were as low as -40°C. So many of the dwellings people lived in were tiny, with as many as 15 family members in either a small ger (Mongolian felt tent) or a small wooden hut. Many of the children had no shoes, very few clothes and often only one or two beds for all of them to share. They had only a candle lit for warmth and a few small bowls of rice for food.*
>
> *My heart ached for these children and adults. "Why, God?" I asked. "Why do they have to go through this suffering?" It dawned on me how privileged I am. Why is it that some are born into this and others are born into a world where they have everything they need? What is my responsibility in this? These were questions I had to ask myself.*
>
> *I began to realise I could bring hope and faith into their situation. I also realised we have a moral responsibility in not just helping people on an emotional and spiritual level, but also helping them in a physical sense.*

So what does that actually mean when we say that? One day two little girls turned up at our place. They were six and eight years old, wearing very thin jackets and sneakers. They were dirty, cold and hungry, saying "Our mum has gone to the city and we don't know what to do or when she will come home. Can we stay with you?" How could we say no? We took them into our home and told them they could stay until their mum returned. But how can a mum just leave her kids like that? Why would a mum leave her kids alone, scared with no one to watch over them?

We found out later she had gone to the city to receive a medal for Motherhood. When you have had a certain number of kids in Mongolia, you receive a medal. It has nothing to do with whether or not you're actually a good parent. The injustice in this made me angry. How can kids suffer like this, yet the country honours the mothers?

In 1990 they discovered a lump on my bladder. It was malignant. I remember feeling anxious as my mum had already gone through cancer. What would this mean for me? Would I be sick for a long time? What if I had to have chemo? Why would God let this happen? It's hard to understand as Christians why we go through suffering; but as Alex shared above, we are not exempt from suffering and pain. In fact, it is through the suffering and pain that we grow and are stretched beyond ourselves, and we recognise our need for God. I was fortunate enough that the doctors were able to remove this cancerous lump and I did not need any further treatment.

Then just before we headed to Mongolia in 1994, I had discovered a small mole on my arm. We prayed it would just go away, but it did not. Did I lack faith, or was God wanting to do something in me through this? After already having had a scare with cancer a few years earlier, I was sure this was going to be okay.

The doctors said it was better to remove it anyway, to be on the safe side. They were pretty sure it was all fine. However, when they did the biopsy, they discovered it was cancerous. I remember feeling shocked and asking God: how could this be? They managed to remove it all and they told me that if they had not done that and we had headed to Mongolia without it being removed, I could have eventually lost my arm.

You see: so often we think we can just pray away hurt and pain and suffering; and while many times we have seen God do the miraculous, we have also seen many times you have to walk through the struggles and learn to find peace with God in the midst of the storms. You have to learn to trust Him in the difficult times.

I'll never forget another time when we were living in Nepal. I had the opportunity to hear an older man speak of the difficulties he had faced. He spoke about the pain and suffering of losing his wife and child. He was from Rwanda and he had watched his wife and child get beheaded in front of him. They had been told to deny Jesus. He was not a believer and he had begged his wife to deny Christ. She looked at him; and said it would be okay.

He said years later after that happened, he came to know Christ. I wondered how a man could choose God with that amount of pain and he went on to share that he didn't know Christ was all he needed until Christ was all he had. I'll never forget the power in that testimony of hearing of his loss and the suffering he went through and yet he went on to become a very strong believer. How does a man choose Christ with having experienced this type of suffering? I have come to understand as Scripture states:

… **'Do not be afraid of what you are about to suffer. I tell you, the devil will put some of you in prison to test you, and you will suffer persecution for ten days. Be faithful, even to the**

point of death, and I will give you life as your victor's crown.' Revelation 2:10 *That is the highest cost of following Jesus, and salvation is worth the joy and hope of what Christ has to offer us.*

Then in 2014 I broke my leg in three places. I was believing for God to heal it straight away. Well, that didn't happen; in fact, I was told that it could be a year or more before I may walk again properly. I was feeling devastated. Yet deep within me, I felt the Lord say that this will be a quicker process than what they are saying.

I had never before been confined to a bed where I had to rely totally on others for everything. I am someone who does not rest well, and the thought of doing nothing but sitting, was not something anyone thought I would be able to do well, least of all me. But somehow in the midst of all the intense pain, the surgery, and the physio, I found peace to trust God.

The next three months I barely left the bed. Alex had to give me injections every day for three months, to ensure I didn't get a blood clot. However, it was in this space God spoke deep into my spirit about keeping my eyes fixed on Him. Trusting God when all is going well is so easy. But trusting God when you are facing some sort of struggle, is often something that we are not prepared for; but have to learn how to journey through it.

At the time I broke my leg, the war on Gaza had just happened. In spite of my pain, I realised that my suffering was nothing compared to the dear ones who had lost homes and watched loved ones die before their very eyes. Suffering comes in all sorts of ways, and I know that God is wanting us to look to Him in the midst of our pain and suffering. Also, we cannot compare our suffering with that of others, as it's different for each of us.

God's promise to us in the midst of all that happens is that we are not alone. We serve a God who is faithful to walk with us through the trials that come our way.

'When you pass through the waters, I will be with you; and when you pass through the rivers, they will not sweep over you. When you walk through the fire, you will not be burned; the flames will not set you ablaze. For I am the Lord your God, the Holy One of Israel, your Saviour.' Isaiah 43:2-4

CHAPTER 9
God's Formula for Faith

Let's be honest: developing a faith that is able to trust God in all circumstances isn't easy. In the previous chapters, we've shared some of the significant steps in our faith journey; but as you have read, we've struggled along the way. It's part of the growing and maturing in God.

In 2020 we bought a house. We weren't planning to buy a house, but Lisa saw this place and it was our dream house. It had a beautiful indoor and outdoor feel, with a central pool and a native forest for a backyard, and had such a peace about it. It was perfect for us. We began to dream of the lifestyle we could have living in this house.

There were many hurdles to be overcome for us to be able to buy the house; not the least being we didn't have enough money! We made an offer and put our old house on the market, believing for God to make it happen, if it was meant to be.

For a number of months, we struggled through the process. We had many encouragements along the way, and several people believed we were meant to have the house; but I struggled to have the faith to believe. After all God had taken us through, here I was stressing about a house.

There are so many facets to faith, but here was one I was not prepared for. I had learnt to have the faith to trust God to decide how to supply our needs, but this was clearly a want not a need. We had put aside chasing after material wants years before. Did God really want us to have this beautiful house?

Friends tried to assure me that we deserved it after all the wild places we had lived in over 25 years serving the Lord; but this just put further doubt in my mind. I felt we didn't deserve anything; we didn't serve the Lord in order that we would get a beautiful house at the end.

Then I began to get a sense from the Lord of the lifestyle we could live in the new place. I began to see how it could be a blessing not only to us, but to others as well. I began to see how God could be in this. But that didn't mean the process was going to be easy.

We struggled through the process. At least twice, it looked as if we had lost the house, and each time the Lord miraculously resurrected the deal. In the end, on the last possible day, the deal was done and there was no doubt it had been the Lord's doing.

Developing a faith that is able to trust God in all circumstances is not an easy process to work through, because circumstances are real. They affect us, they can cause us anxiety and pain; but fortunately the Bible gives us instructions on the steps of how to do it.

Proverbs 3:5-6 says, "**Trust in the Lord with all your heart and lean not on your own understanding; in all your ways submit to him, and he will make your paths straight.**"

Let's break this down step by step...

Step 1

Trust in the Lord with all of your heart

In the earlier chapters, we have discussed in depth the importance of developing a faith based on being able to look beyond circumstances to trust in the person of God; so there is no need to repeat it here.

Suffice to say that trusting in the Lord is having faith in who God is, not in the circumstances. It's focusing our eyes on him. It's believing God is bigger than our circumstances. It's understanding that God is sovereign in all situations and that He cares deeply about us and about our situation; remembering that he is compassionate and gracious, slow to anger, abounding in love. (Psalm 103:8)

Step 2

Lean not on your own understanding

It's natural for us to want to try and make sense of the world around us, to try to understand what is happening and why it's happening. You could say our modern society is built on scientific discovery: the process of understanding the "what and why" in life. While this has led to many great advances in technology, not to mention that now with a click of a button, I can watch any of my all-time favourite movies whenever I want to; it has come at a cost.

The cost is the loss of mystery. As our collective knowledge increases, the world and life become less mysterious. We become less and less comfortable with mystery. We feel we should understand everything and that we have a right to know.

But to unlock faith, we have to learn to put aside our understanding and look to the mystery of God. It's so counter-cultural to modern society; but we have to bring back the mystery. We have to embrace the mystery of God and how he works in our lives.

In Matthew 19:23-24 Jesus said… **'Truly I tell you, it is hard for someone who is rich to enter the kingdom of heaven. Again I tell you, it is easier for a camel to go through the eye of a needle than for someone who is rich to enter the kingdom of God.'**

I think modern well-educated 'scientific thinkers' have the same problem.

Walking in faith is all about being prepared to stop leaning on our understanding and to embrace the mystery of God at work in our lives.

Step 3

In all of your ways submit to Him

In Arabic there's a phrase that's commonly used in daily life 'Inshallah'. (Pronounced as in-shal-lah) It's an expression for "God willing" or "if God wills". The phrase comes from a Quranic command which commands Muslims to use it when speaking of future events. While for Muslims it can carry a very fatalistic view of future events, I found that when working alongside Muslim colleagues, the phrase became part of my vocabulary, and it challenged me daily. Was I really willing to submit every part of my life to the Lord? Was I serious about what I was saying?

Submission is where the rubber hits the road, as they say. It's where following Jesus gets real. When we first begin to follow Jesus and take our first steps, we experience a certain level of submission. We acknowledge Jesus as the son of God, as our Saviour and we accept the Lordship of Jesus over our lives.

However; I have found this is just the beginning of the submission journey, not the end.

We love having people to our home. One, two, ten or twenty; the more the merrier. We love the sound of laughter and of people relaxing around the pool and having a good time.

While I'm very comfortable to have people come into our kitchen or lounge because they're always tidy, I might be a bit worried if you wanted to come into our bedroom if we hadn't made the bed and I would really struggle if you wanted to go into my teenage sons bedroom because who knows what state that might be in.

Our lives can be a bit like our houses. One room could be work, one could be family, one could be self, our personal habits etc. And while we are comfortable to submit some areas to God, others we are nervous about submitting and some we really struggle to submit.

These areas we struggle to submit can be because of issues of old habits and sin that hasn't been dealt with or just about learning to trust God.

There's no shortcuts or easy fixes here. The reality is simply that the more of our lives we can submit to God, the freer we become from the chains of circumstances that would stop us from walking in faith.

Step 4

And He will make your paths straight

If the tough news is that there is no way around the issue of submission, the good news is that God has provided a way.

We struggle to submit areas of our lives to God because we fear what may happen. We're afraid because of the shame and pain of our brokenness. We would rather hold on to our brokenness than let the Divine Healer do spiritual surgery: like a person putting up with a painful boil, rather than letting the doctor lance it.

For those willing to take the step of faith and invite God into these areas, the results are nothing less than miraculous.

Lisa and I now work with families in South Auckland. Many of the family members we work with have a background of drug addiction, domestic violence, and sexual abuse, child abandonment, living on the streets, gang affiliation, and crime and prison time. All have struggled with serious trauma from the time they were children. As they open up and allow God to enter their lives, it's wonderful to see, how He brings healing and transformation.

As we submit to God, He takes our crooked, twisted, messed up paths and gently, lovingly straightens them. As we hand over control to Him; our Heavenly Father who loves us begins to direct events according to His will. With all of his deep, deep love for us, He uses all of His all-knowing omniscience and all of his all-powerful omnipotence to make our paths straight as only he can do.

Trusting in the Lord, leaning not on your own understanding; submitting to him, and He will make your paths straight. This is God's formula for faith. The more we practise it, the more our faith grows.

CHAPTER 10

A Supernatural Experience

I've been a fan of the writer JRR Tolkien since I was 15 years old, when I discovered his book "The Hobbit".

Page after page, I found myself drawn to the journey and adventures of the little hobbits as they made their way across Middle Earth. Page after page, I found myself drawn to the lure of the road, longing for the freedom of stepping away from the normal and mundane, and impatient for the excitement and uncertainty of adventure. Deep within me was a realisation that I was not created to remain in one place, bound by the familiar. I was created for the open road. I was created for the journey.

Having read this far, you could be thinking our journey and calling has been a little extreme and thankfully this is not you; but I'm convinced we are all created to journey. It's just the type of journey that's different for each of us.

Journey without end

Unlike a book which eventually comes to an end, our spiritual journey has no end. There is always a new chapter to explore. God always has new revelations and new faith challenges for us to overcome, as we journey deeper and deeper with Him.

God's invitation to us has always been to journey with Him. In the Book of Genesis chapter three, we read of God walking in the garden in the cool of the day.

'Then the man and his wife heard the sound of the Lord God as he was walking in the garden in the cool of the day, and they hid from the Lord God among the trees of the garden.' Genesis 3:8

God wasn't in the garden walking for His health. God didn't need an evening constitutional or power walk to keep fit. It was an invitation to Adam and Eve to walk together. The invitation has always been there; it's only our sin and our fallen nature which prevents us journeying together.

Our sin and fallen nature will always try to separate us from the presence of God, just like it did with Adam and Eve. It will pull us into distractions and busyness, or in our pride, try to convince us we've journeyed enough; that we've made it; that we've reached 'the' level, whatever 'the' level is.

Faith is not like a computer game where we go level by level, grabbing the bonuses until we reach the final level. There is no final level. Even death is only a transition to the next chapter of the journey.

Take a moment to think about it and reflect. If we have an eternal spirit, we're following an eternal, everlasting God, and there is no end to God, then how can our journey with Him ever end?

Walking in faith

I hear believers talking about being bored with their spiritual walk saying... "Eh.... I've read the Bible and I'm not interested in reading it again .... I'm tired of praying the same old prayers ... I'm bored with Church; it's not entertaining enough".

If this is you: in love, I want to shout out to you WAKE UP! You're MISSING THE WHOLE POINT!

You're missing the excitement of walking daily by faith; and being balanced on the knife edge of uncertain possibility. You're missing the thrill of living as a vessel that daily God pours His supernatural power through us to perform miracles, signs and wonders.

Sadly, there are two kinds of believers in this world; those who get out of bed in the morning to a mundane, natural, predictable life of just going through the motions; and those who get up out of bed each day to a life of a supernatural superhero living, a life of supernatural adventure.

Walking by faith is what transforms our daily natural life into a supernatural adventure.

We were born to be supernatural superheroes, with faith as our superpower. Sorry; my twelve-year-old son is crazy about superheroes, and I get fed a steady diet of Marvel superheroes at the moment; so I'm getting carried away with the 'super' metaphors... but I hope you get what I mean.

We were born for such a time as this, and it is an exciting time to be alive.

Jesus said, "Very truly I tell you, whoever believes in me will do the works I have been doing, and they will do even greater things than these…" John 14:12

As believers, when we walk by faith, we step into the footprints of Jesus. This is the key that unlocks our birth right and all of the supernatural power of heaven is available to us. It is something that never stops.

Three years ago, God called me to lay down the international humanitarian ministry and step into a new chapter as associate pastor in a local church in South Auckland. We were grateful for the opportunity; but it was a real step of faith. It was something I thought I would never do. After the journey we had been on, what would I do as a local pastor?

What we have found is that we are not called to take the occasional step of faith. We are called to walk in faith, day by day, for our entire lives. As long as we are willing to walk in faith, God will continue to lead us into new chapters in our lives.

I went into the role saying, "God, whatever this new role brings, I'm open to it". Sometimes I forget that God takes us at our word; and He has a great sense of humour. The very first thing I was asked to do was start a men's ministry. Oh God; why that? I've never been a 'men's group' type of guy. Do I look as if I need male-bonding?

During the times I've lived in a country where there was a men's group, I've avoided them like the plague. I don't know why; I've just never been comfortable with them. I guess that in New Zealand I don't follow sport closely enough to know who's doing well and who's out the back door and this seems to be the basis of most men's conversations at men's groups. Men's ministry; really?

I said I would do anything; so now I needed to step up in faith. If I was going to do this and stay sane, I would have to do it in a way I could engage my passion for working with people on the edge.

It's true there's no bombing, rioting or civil war on the streets of South Auckland, but there is plenty of destruction in families and in the lives of men. Anger, frustration, poverty, alcohol, drugs, domestic violence, gangs, crime and prison all destroy the lives of men and their families.

If we were going to have a men's ministry, then let's have one that would matter, that would make a difference. So in faith, I focused the group on men at risk, believing in faith that somehow we could create a group that would make a difference in men's lives.

The first couple of years was challenging. We saw men come into the group and come into a relationship with Jesus. Some experienced immediate supernatural transformation, turning from anger, violence, drug addiction etc. For many, though, it was a struggle to work through the process of change.

We continued to journey with the guys, and by the third year we saw something incredible begin to happen. These new believers who had come from such difficult backgrounds and had to fight hard to overcome the past, were already beginning to step out naturally and walk by faith.

Each week at our meetings we would have a time of 'God Stories', where men could share what God had done during the week. At the start of the third year, the stories shifted from how God had helped them get through the week, to how they had stepped out in faith and God had used them. Some of these men had only been believers for six months.

One of the guys, who had left the gang life, was invited to go and speak to a national meeting of his old gang. He told them that if he did, he would be talking about Jesus; which, incredibly, they agreed to. He spoke out courageously and many men made decisions to follow Jesus.

Another of the guys was in a dairy (a small corner store), buying something when two armed men burst in to rob the shop keeper. Feeling prompted by the Holy Spirit, he interrupted the robbers to boldly tell them both that they didn't need cash, but they needed the transforming power of Jesus and could he pray for them. One of the guys told him to get lost but the other one broke down and asked for him to pray. Incredibly, when the police arrived, they arrested the guy who refused Jesus and let the one who accepted Jesus go.

Another time a sister of one of the guys was suffering terminal cancer and he went to the hospital to the 'terminal ward', where patients in the last stages of terminal cancer are cared for. Again, the Holy Spirit prompted him and he stepped out in faith, singing to the patients and praying for them. I'm not sure what happened to the other patients; but a short time later, we learnt his sister had made a full recovery, which the doctors couldn't explain.

And so on and so on.

These are not guys you would normally expect to see in 'Christian ministry'. They came from really messed-up backgrounds and were young in their spiritual journeys. They were not appointed by the church into positions of ministry; but they were willing to step up, and God brought them into a place of supernatural adventure. This is what happens when we walk in faith.

These stories from the men's group are some stories of what can happen when we walk by faith, but what else does walking by faith look like?

It looks like opening our hearts and really surrendering our lives to Jesus. To begin to walk the spiritual journey of faith, we need to really surrender our self-reliance, our pride, and our ambitions. Too often we play at surrender. We put God in the driver's seat in our lives and then daily try to wrestle the steering wheel back off Him. No wonder we crash from time to time. Or more correctly God, releases the wheel to us, and we crash.

Available for adventure

I've come to believe that sometimes in the western evangelical church, we focus too much on what our "giftings" are or what we are 'qualified' to do. We get so carried away with what we are not gifted or qualified to do, that we start to tell God what we're available to do, rather than coming before Him open and ready to receive our instructions. When given an opportunity to share the Gospel with someone searching for truth, how often do we hear the excuse "I'm not an evangelist? It's not my gifting". If we're not careful, it can become another way of wrestling the steering wheel off God.

Where in the Bible do we read of God using gifted or qualified people to do His will? Abraham was too old, Sarah was impatient, Isaac was a daydreamer, Jacob was a cheater, Noah got drunk, Jonah ran from God, Moses stuttered, Gideon was insecure, David was an adulterer and tried to cover it up with murder, Elijah was moody and suicidal, Rahab was a prostitute, Peter had a temper and denied Christ, Paul was a murderer, Timothy had too many ulcers, Miriam was a gossiper, Thomas was a doubter, Zacchaeus oppressed the poor and cheated people. The one thing they all had in common was that they were willing to surrender their lives and be available for God.

We see this even in the life of the great prophet Isaiah, when he writes in the Book of Isaiah chapter 6:5-8:

"Woe to me!" I cried. "I am ruined! For I am a man of unclean lips, and I live among a people of unclean lips, and my eyes have seen the King, the Lord Almighty. Then one of the seraphim flew to me with

a live coal in his hand, which he had taken with tongs from the altar. With it he touched my mouth and said, "See, this has touched your lips; your guilt is taken away and your sin atoned for. Then I heard the voice of the Lord saying, "Whom shall I send? And who will go for us? And I said, "Here am I. Send me!"

Surrender opens the door of opportunity with God. If we had waited to start our journey until we felt sufficiently gifted or qualified, we would still be waiting, waiting, and waiting... Don't fall into the devil's trap and delay, delay, delay; when the Bible teaches, "Choose TODAY[6] whom will you serve." Make that decision, come over the line, commit.

Surrender is being ready each day for divine appointments: those moments when the opportunity to be the hands and feet of God are there to be seized. You may have the opportunity to speak into the lives of those in desperate need of the transforming power of Jesus or to pray for healing or speak life through a word of encouragement. You will be sharing the reality of God's love.

There are a few things we've found that can help us to walk by faith. The first is: we need to know the character of God.

Knowing the One we journey with

It's so much easier to trust someone you know, rather than a stranger. For example, if a stranger said "You need to come with me now and get in my car. Don't worry, I'll tell you what it's about on the way". Would you do it? Or would you hesitate, or even refuse?

I would certainly hesitate and probably refuse. But if Lisa my wife said the same thing, I'd jump right in without hesitation. Why? Because I know and trust her.

---

6. Joshua 24:15

Psalm 9:10 speaks of this. 'Those who know your name trust in you, for you, Lord, have never forsaken those who seek you.'

To walk daily in faith, we need to really get to know who Jesus is. We need to get past the stereotypes and two-dimensional caricatures. We need to explore the different dimensions of who He is.

I remember the first impression I had of my wife Lisa. This glowing, angelic, stunning looking woman with her 80's permed hair, beautiful smile and infectious laugh. Yes, these were all aspects of her; but as I was to discover as our relationship went deeper, there was much, much more to her. I discovered her heart, her natural kindness, her instinct to put others ahead of herself. I found her deep commitment to relationship and readiness to say sorry, even when it should be me apologising. I also discovered she has a steel-like determination, a tendency to push herself beyond her limits; and she has little tolerance for 'man flu'. Is that a female thing?

The point is: when I started a relationship with her, it was only the tip of the iceberg. It was what first attracted me, but it was not enough to build a trusting relationship on.

I have more trust and faith in my wife than in any other person I know, because for 35 years, as we have related to each other and journeyed together, I have been able to explore all the different aspects of her personality and character. I know what she thinks about different subjects and so on.

Unfortunately, too often we don't do this with God. We seem satisfied to remain with the simplified Sunday school or new believer understanding of who He is, and not go deeper.

So many times, in counselling people about issues of faith, I see that the root of their struggle is a false understanding of who God is. He gets such a bad rap. He's seen as this distant, angry guy sitting on a huge throne with an impressive frown on His face, and He's always somehow disappointed with us, because we can never seem to get it totally right. Because of His goodness, He continues to tolerate us; and if we could just do a bit more, we might be able to earn His love. But we know deep down inside, we're still struggling with our sinful nature, so it's all hopeless really… This is the good news of the Gospel?

No! Wrong! Wrong! Wrong!

If this is your idea of God, then it's time to put away those old Renaissance art pictures in your mind; the angry caricatures. It's time for you to encounter who God really is. Yes, He is holy and righteous, but He is also loving, joyous, peaceful, patient, kind, good, faithful, gentle, full of self-control; and has the best sense of humour of anyone.

Not only is God all these things, but He is the source of these things. That's why we call them the *fruit* of the Holy Spirit as we read in Galatians 5:22-23…

'But the fruit of the Spirit is love, joy, peace, forbearance, kindness, goodness, faithfulness, gentleness and self-control. Against such things there is no law.'

How do we get to know the real character and nature of God? Two ways I have found.

First, by reading the Bible through the lens of discovering who God is, particularly focusing on Jesus in the gospels of the New Testament, as the final progressive revelation of God. What does each passage tell me about who God is? What's God doing? Why is He doing it? What is He thinking and feeling?

The second is by spending time with Him; spending time in relationship with Him.

As we spend more and more time with Him, we get to know Him in a much deeper way, and we get better at hearing His voice, after a while we begin to really know the voice of our Saviour.

Jesus said in the book of John 10:27 **"My sheep know my voice; I know them, and they follow me"**. Knowing the voice of our shepherd, is what we need to be able to follow Him.

In New Zealand we use dogs to shepherd sheep. They bark and drive the sheep towards where they need to go; but it's different in the Middle East. I remember seeing the shepherds many times in Palestine, leading not driving their sheep. They call to their sheep and the sheep know the sound of their shepherd's voice. So even if two herds get mixed up during the day, at night when it's time to head home, all the shepherd needs to do is call out and the sheep know which is their shepherd by the sound of his voice.

Relationship, real relationship, where we really know who God is, is so important to God that it's the measure He uses to judge who are really His followers.

"Not everyone who says to me, 'Lord, Lord,' will enter the kingdom of heaven, but only the one who does the will of my Father who is in heaven. Many will say to me on that day, 'Lord, Lord, did we not prophesy in your name and in your name drive out demons, and in your name perform many miracles?' Then I will tell them plainly, 'I never knew you. Away from me, you evildoers!' Matthew 7: 21-23

Perhaps the most important thing about walking by faith is actually seeing our self as someone who walks by faith, rejecting our self-doubt and insecurity. We need to turn off the tapes in our head that say we are nothing, we can't do it, or who are we to make a difference.

We were created for a purpose. It's no accident I was born at this time and this place. It's no accident you were born at this time and this place. One of the greatest milestones in my life's journey was when I realised that I actually believed this.

It's a huge game-changer. It means that what I do or don't do matters. It means I don't live in some kind of anonymous vacuum. I can affect the world around me, and the lives of those people God brings across my path. If I am walking in faith, God can use me: I really can be the hands and feet of God.

All those who journey share two things in common: a dissatisfaction for where I am at present and a passion for what is over the horizon. I pray for us all to have a holy dissatisfaction for where our faith is at present, and a passion to continually explore new horizons of faith.

Thank you for taking the time to journey with us through the pages of this book. I trust that through the experiences and lessons we have shared, your own faith has been challenged and you have been encouraged to continue your own faith journey.

Lisa and I would like to leave you with the beautiful words of a prayer in Te Rao Maori, the indigenous language of Aotearoa New Zealand, which is often used to bring a time of being together to an end.

Let's pray together:

Kia tau ki a tātou katoa,
te atawhai o tō tātou Ariki aa Ihu Karaiti
me te aroha o te Atua
me te whiwhinga tahitanga
ki te Wairua Tapu.
Āke, āke, āke,
Amine

May the grace of the Lord Jesus Christ,
And the love of God
And the fellowship of the Holy Spirit,
Be with you all
Forever and ever.

Amen
(The prayer was written in reference to 2 Corinthians 13:14)

ALEX, LISA, MONQTUYA AND ZAC - 2020

Contact the author by emailing to

snaryauthors@gmail.com

Social Media
Facebook.com/alexandlisasnary

INSPIRED TO WRITE A BOOK?

Contact

Maurice Wylie Media
Inspirational Christian Publisher

Based in Northern Ireland and distributing around the world.
www.MauriceWylieMedia.com

www.ingramcontent.com/pod-product-compliance
Lightning Source LLC
Chambersburg PA
CBHW071616080526
44588CB00010B/1151